LOTUS BIRTH

Dear Noor,

love and many

blessings & enjoy!

Shivam Rachana

Lotus Birth

compiled by Shivam Rachana

Greenwood Press, Steels Creek, Australia

First published 2000
by Greenwood Press
PO Box 233, Yarra Glen, Victoria 3775, Australia

Lotus Birth
ISBN 0 646 40652 3

Edited by Soni Stecker
Design and layout by Bill Potter
Cover design by Leanne Kirkman
(based on an idea by Isolde Malga)
Cover photo of Madeleine by Simone Lukacs
Printed in Australia by The Craftsman Press Pty Ltd, Burwood, Victoria

CIP data
1. Natural childbirth.
I. Rachana, Shivam.
618.45

The method of postpartum care presented in this book should be viewed as an option for careful consideration. Any application of the ideas, suggestions, and procedures described are at the reader's own discretion.

Dedication

This book is dedicated to the late
Dr Graham Farrant,
whose ground-breaking work enabled me to
heal and inspired me to trust, trust deeply the
unspoken/unspeakable;

and
to the children of the future

Lotus Birth is the practice of leaving the umbilical cord uncut, so that the baby remains attached to the placenta until the cord naturally separates at the navel – exactly as a cut cord does – at three to ten days after birth. This prolonged contact can be seen as a time of transition, allowing the baby to slowly and gently let go of the attachment to the mother's body.

Dr Sarah Buckley, *Pregnancy* magazine, Spring 1998

Lotus Birth is part of the continuum in the development and unfolding of the human organism.

Lotus Birth is also part of the continuum of awakening consciousness expressing itself via the birth process.

Foreword

WHEN Shivam Rachana first told me about the concept of Lotus Birth, I was intrigued by such an unexpected association of words. After a while I started to visualise lotus flowers blooming on calm water. I then understood why the lotus has always been deemed the primary flower and the symbol of the appearance of life. Suddenly I had access to an interpretation of the concept of Lotus Birth.

We are at a time in the history of humankind when human groups need to invent radically new strategies for survival. For millennia all cultures have shared the same basic strategies: to dominate nature and to dominate, or even to eliminate, other human groups. It was an advantage to develop the human potential for aggressiveness, to develop a certain capacity to destroy life, and therefore to control the capacity to love. In the age of the 'scientification of love' we are learning how the capacity to love develops. By weaving together data offered by multiple scientific perspectives, we can reach the conclusion that the period surrounding birth is critical. Today we are in a position to interpret the evolutionary advantages of the countless rituals and beliefs (e.g. 'the colostrum is bad') that have been transmitted over millennia and that tend to disturb the birth itself and the first contact between mother and baby.

The limits of such strategies are obvious in the age of ecological awareness. We need to raise radically new questions such as: 'How do we develop respect for Mother Earth?' The unification of humanity is a necessary step for a dialogue with Mother Earth. We need the energies of Love. All the beliefs and rituals interfering with the physiological processes in the critical period surrounding birth are losing their evolutionary advantages. We need to re-learn what a birth can be like when it is not disturbed by the cultural milieu. We need a reference point from which we should try not to deviate too much. *Lotus Birth is such a reference point.*

There are two complementary ways to go back to the roots where childbirth is concerned. One is to penetrate ancient women's knowledge, which is still alive in spite of millennia of culture. Shivam Rachana and her friends of the International College of Spiritual Midwifery are well advanced in exploring that way. The other one is to use the perspective of modern physiologists in order to identify what is really universal and to rediscover the basic needs of labouring women.

If we visualise a labouring woman with the eyes of a physiologist, we visualise the deep part of her brain as the most active part of her body: old structures we share with all other mammals (hypothalamus, pituitary gland, etc.) must release the necessary hormones. If there are inhibitions, they originate in that part of the brain that is so highly developed among humans: the neocortex. The cultural conditioning is imprinted in this new brain, which can be presented also as the brain of the intellect. From the perspective of a physiologist it is easy to interpret a phenomenon which is well known by 'spiritual midwives'. When a woman is in undisturbed labour, she is is in a specific state of consciousness, as if cutting herself from our world and 'going to another planet'. She dares to do what would be unacceptable in her daily life: for example she might scream or swear, or she might be in a posture she had never anticipated. This means that her neocortex is reducing its activity. This reduction of the neocortical control is the only important aspect of birth physiology from a practical point of view. It implies that the basic need of a labouring woman is to be protected against any sort of neocortical stimulation. For physiologists the watchword is: do not stimulate the neocortex of a labouring woman.

What can stimulate the neocortex of a human being?

Language is processed by the neortex. This means that labouring women should not be exposed to unnecessary words. Bright lights stimulate the neocortex. This means that there is a qualitative difference between a dim light and a bright light in a birthing place. Any situation when one feels observed tends to stimulate the neocortex. This means that privacy is a basic need. Any situation associated with an increased level of adrenaline tends also to stimulate the neocortex. This implies that to feel secure is another basic need of labouring women. Let us underline that our mother is the prototype of the person with whom we feel secure and that a midwife is originally a mother figure.

With the perspective of physiologists, it is easy to rediscover the basic and universal needs of a woman giving birth. Furthermore, with the language of physiologists, it is easy to evaluate the deep-rooted and widespread misunderstanding of birth physiology.

The gap between the intuitive knowledge certain women still have and what we can learn from biological sciences is becoming narrower and narrower. There are reasons for optimism.

Michel Odent
London, October 2000

French obstetrician and natural birthing methods pioneer
Founder, Primal Health Research Centre, London

Acknowledgments

This book has come into being with the loving help of many people. I thank Soni Stecker, my editor, for her constant midwifing me through times of unclarity and uncertainty into order and completion. Many thanks to Marg Potter for many hours of typing, Carolyn Tucker for her precise drawings, Sarah Buckley for her collaboration, her photos and for compiling the list of further reading. Thanks also to Bill Potter for his text design, Isolde Malga for the inspiration of the front cover and Leanne Kirkman for the cover design, and Simone Lukacs and Davini Joy for the photos of their children. My thanks go to the many contributors for the stories and insights they have shared – they are true trailblazers for a new generation of children. My gratitude to my son Sean and daughter Bree, whose births and lives have instructed me deeply, and to my sister Kushna Warszewski, who dared to be the first and enabled others to follow. I am grateful to Sunderai Felich and Anand Khushi for their friendship and constant assistance over the years, and to my beloved husband Deva Daricha for his care, encouragement and forbearance. And last but not least, a million thanks to all the children who continue to point the way.

Shivam Rachana

Contents

Chapter 9: Midwives' experiences with Lotus Birth

Introduction

Shivam Rachana

Placenta – Latin, from the Greek *plakous ountos,*
meaning flat cake.
From root: *plax plakos,* meaning flat plate.

Each year, on the anniversary of our birth – our birthday – it is customary in Western culture to have a cake,
served on a flat plate, decorated with lit candles. We have a
birthday song sung to us, we blow out the candles, we are
clapped and cheered, we stab the cake (without touching
the bottom), we cut it and share it with others to eat.

If the knife is dirty the nearest girl or boy may be
kissed. This sets in motion again the dance of creation,
where it all began. A tier of the wedding cake is often kept
for the birth of the first child.

Even in our modern culture, so devoid of ritual, we
enshrine a sense of devotion to and celebration of the
sacred placenta through these customs.

I T was in 1979, while undergoing primal therapy, that I first
became aware of the pain and trauma of having my umbilical
cord cut when I was born. I had been fortunate to have the
opportunity to work with Dr Graham Farrant in Melbourne and to

re-experience – or relive – early events, particularly the events of my own birth and intrauterine experience. This has provided me with a wealth of insights into my perceived sense of reality and the deeply hidden forces that lived in me, influencing my responses and behaviours. It was a major developmental point in my life for which I am most grateful.

Having my cord cut hurt. My stomach ached and throbbed like an enormous heart. I was angry and most distressed – I knew it wasn't necessary and felt, 'how dare they!'. During subsequent sessions I revisited my cord cutting and released pains that I had carried all my life. Being drugged when I was born – via the anaesthestic given to my mother – I had not had access to my own feelings at that time. One day, having processed more cord trauma, I found myself hugging a pillow. It flashed into my mind that this was my placenta. I hadn't previously thought about my placenta – I had been locked into the pain of having the cord cut at my navel. That was the site of the pain. But here I was with my placenta and I felt so amazingly well, so very okay, such joy and mirth – such a feeling of possession, a wholeness. I cuddled it and humped it around like I've seen children do with favourite blankets. It was a feeling I could not remember having experienced before.

I remained, curled up, clutching my dear placenta pillow, without a care in the world – complete in a most organic way. At one point somebody passed by where it was and I remember thinking: 'If they try to take it from me, I'll kill them'. The intensity of this surprised me; however, it certainly was how I felt. After some time – around one-and-a-half hours or so – I felt a shift in my awareness and I came out of that state and the pillow was suddenly a pillow and I simply left it where it was and moved on, aware that something had changed within me.

At that time I had become obsessively dependent on my diary. It was a source of reference to my very existence. Everything I was to do was recorded in 'The Diary'. It was most important to me. That was my life! In about June/July for the previous couple of years I had lost my diary, and along with it my sense of purpose. It had become my reality check. It was always a major business, the searching for and the mourning of the lost diary and finally the purchasing of another; then replacing lost data. Since my time with the placenta pillow I haven't lost a diary.

My handbag and I were also always a real team. We were always together. Indeed I would feel incomplete without my handbag – in it were all the things I needed, or so I believed. I couldn't manage without it. Since my time with the placenta pillow I am at ease and often prefer to be without a handbag and find that mostly I manage easily.

People create all sorts of attachments. The diary and handbag are quite common ones. For children it is often a soft toy or a 'special something' that they need to have with them at sleep time. Have you noticed people and their pets? Pets often display the characteristics of their owners, appear as an extension of the humans. They are often on the end of a leash (cord) – these soft warm-blooded companionable creatures. Was our placenta our first companion?

My primal therapy experiences were rich opportunities for deepening and widening my knowledge and understanding of the birth process.

The discovery that my own birth had been an induced, drugged, forceps delivery thirty years before gave me some explanation as to how it had been repeated in the birth of my first-born, despite my every effort and wish for a natural birth. The primal imprint of my own birth drove deep unconscious forces within me to what in some ways was an inevitable outcome – disaster. How deep these forces are. My son became the third generation of first-born males to have a horrifically traumatic birth. I joined my mother and grandmother in having my beautiful body slashed and bruised at the hands of the medical profession – healthy women reduced to infirm patients in recovery, with a new baby to care for.

Home births were becoming very popular among people I knew and I was fortunate to have the opportunity to attend some. Seeing babies born at home showed me the normality of birth. It was simply normal and sacred and exciting at the same time. Both my parents had been born at home and I reached back through my son's and my own birth to be reconnected to this normal behaviour. It was very healing for me, and nine months after attending my first home birth I reclaimed that normal behaviour by birthing my second child in the bed where she had been conceived.

Working with people preparing for birth and attending births became part of my life. Most families I attended practised the procedures recommended by the French obstetrician, Leboyer, who saw the light after re-experiencing his own birth. Lights were dim, people quietly supporting the mother, the babies were born drug free and placed on their mother's abdomen. The umbilical cord was left until it had stopped pulsating – usually 20 minutes or more – before it was cut. Sometimes the placenta had delivered and often it delivered after the cord was cut. The baby was floated in a bath of warm water and we would watch in awe as the tension fell away and the little one's body opened like a magnificent flower, the baby often smiling. Water births were yet to be on the scene.

From our primal experiences we had come to understand how our own births influenced how we reacted and responded when attending births. Viewed through the filter of our own trauma, our interpretation of what was happening was likely to be inaccurate. We learnt to be aware of our own feelings and to be present for the mother and baby with clarity.

In studying our behaviour we came to see the value of minimal interference from outside the sacred triad of mother–father–baby. Pregnancy and birth are a time of personal development and maturation. There are many points when the couple either step into their own power and grow, or are thwarted by others who take initiatives that are not really theirs to take. While I won't list all those possible occasions here, I will mention some post-birth protocols that I have developed to support this process.

The discovery of the baby's sex is, I think, the parents' prerogative and it is important that due respect is paid so that they can do it in their own way. This often allows a baby to be welcomed as a being in its own right, before being categorised 'girl' or 'boy' with all the cultural expectations associated with it. I have seen instances when one or both parents have had a particular preference for a girl or a boy. Then, when the baby is greeted and met without that information, by the time the parents do discover the sex a point of resolution has been arrived at, because they have fallen in love with the baby. Something that had previously been an issue no longer exists and they are delighted with what they discover.

We ensure where possible that the first voices the baby hears and the first faces she or he looks upon are those of the mother and father. Recent research indicates that the first 45 minutes are vital for the establishment of the flow of oxytocin, which contributes to the baby's neurological development and sense of wellbeing. This is a time for the mother and child, not strangers. The long-term implications of disruption of this process are continuing to be revealed as we appreciate more fully the precision of nature's design and the wisdom of supporting it.

I began to notice that often babies who were very quiet would begin to cry when their cord was cut. They would be very distressed, sometimes crying for more than 30 minutes. The question arose: 'Does the baby know about its placenta?' and 'Does the cutting of the cord hurt it?' There is now a growing body of evidence to support the view that babies do, indeed, have full awareness at birth (unless they are drugged) and that they do feel pain.

In the births I attended, by and large the care provided was non-interventionist for first and second stage of labour. Mothers went into labour spontaneously; there were minimal, if any, internal examinations and only rare rupture of membranes. The foetal heart was monitored as unobstructively as possible. Analgesia or forceps were very rare. Once the cord was cut, however, there was quite a bit of sudden 'doing'. If the placenta hadn't delivered there was a tendency to apply cord traction (i.e. the doctor or midwife would pull on the cord) to encourage the placenta to deliver, or pressure was applied to the mother's stomach. Both were invariably unpleasant for the mother. There was a prevailing anxiety about postpartum haemorrage. This would vary between practitioners. The natural wish to finish up and go home, which is very understandable, also played a part.

Taught procedure was that the placenta had to be inspected, measured and weighed and these figures recorded. A complete placenta meant that there were no retained pieces in the uterus. This was part of the required 'standard of care'.

We had found that by abandoning many intrusive procedures in first and second stage that accounted for 'required standard of care' elsewhere, we were getting wonderful outcomes as the mothers connected with their own mammalian knowing and birthed their babies triumphantly. Third stage had not had such attention – yet.

The children

A potent source of information for me were young children. It was not unusual for children to be at the births that took place at home. In their play a toy with a cord or pull-along of some sort would very often become a coveted possession. The toy telephone was probably the toy most fought over. There would be calls of 'It's mine! I want it! Give it to me! It's not fair!' and tears of loss and grief.

A three-year-old boy, neighbour of a two-and-a-half-year-old girl, came to her house the morning after her baby brother was born. She ran and greeted her friend and took his hand. I watched them, expecting her to take him to see the new baby, but she took him to the bucket where the placenta lay. The two of them stood there, wordless, hand in hand; there was a deep silence as they looked and were simply 'with' the placenta. 'Why did they do that?', I wondered. It was obviously meaningful for them.

Over time the children kept me on track. There was a point when I was doubting the whole placenta 'business' and thought it had become obsessive, that maybe I should let it go. I attended a post-birth get together. Gathered were those who had been present – this included children aged from six months to eight years. It was a time to share stories and also look at photos. There were a lot of photos. One of the women was a professional photographer and the shots were stunning. She put them all out for us to see and told the kids to chose the one they'd like and she would have a copy made for them. Each child (apart from the six-month old) chose the photo of the placenta! It was definitely a sign for me to keep going with my quest.

We decided to apply the 'mother leads' principle to third stage – we would wait for the mother to determine the time the cord would be cut. So babies were born, placentas would follow, usually 20 to 30 minutes, sometimes much later; the babies would rest with the placenta beside them. It would be about one-and-a-half hours after the birth that the mothers would mention the cord. And it would often be in the way of a question: 'Shall we cut the cord now?', not a directive: 'Now cut the cord'.

As we had no other possibility in our yet to be expanded minds we would say 'yes' and the cord would be cut. Some babies would fuss and cry. It was obvious to us that the baby was conscious of the cord and its connection to it.

The next step in our evolution was to speak to the baby, once the mother had queried us. We or she would say to the baby: 'We are going to cut your cord now – is that okay with you?' This would usually be one and a half hours after the birth. Some babies seemed fine with this and the cord was cut. However, a notable number would respond with squirming, fretting, reaching out and holding onto the cord. One little fellow I saw began to wring his tiny hands. Another reached out and pushed away at the hand that held the scissors that were to be used. We were amazed!

In 1982 I compiled a research questionnaire on third stage that provided me with some very valuable information. I presented it at a seminar attended by pregnant couples, midwives, childbirth educators and doulas. Research had been conducted among 153 women on their and their babies' experiences of third stage in the hospital environment. The data collected found that procedures and interventions that were routinely carried out caused discomfort and distress for both mother and baby.

The survey showed a dramatic relationship between the time the cord was cut after birth and the number of days it took for the navel to heal.

Time the cord was cut	Time required for the navel to heal
immediately	9.56 days
when pulsing stopped	7.16 days
later	3.75 days

Another interesting point was who initiated the cutting of the cord, as demonstrated in the following table:

Initiator	Percentage
Doctor	68%
Midwife	22%
Father	7%
Mother	3%

This is interesting when you consider that in all other mammals the mother in 100% of cases initiates the severing of the cord and then ingests the afterbirth, keeping it in the mother–baby unit. The nutrients are being passed on to the baby via feeding.

Reported reactions of babies to having their cords cut included: 'gasped, shuddered, screamed, cried louder, whimpered, wringing of hands, began crying'. Mothers' descriptions of third stage included: 'unpleasant, didn't notice, awful, horrific, a non-experience, foggy, pretty dreadful, disastrous, painful, surprising, lovely, sensuous'.

At the seminar the midwives who rarely cut cords until well after the placenta delivered spoke of the natural evolution and successful completion of third stage. Third stage was discussed as a time of potential healing on physical and spiritual levels for the mother and the baby; a time of resolution after the excitement of birth and before the beginning of the fourth stage as mothers, sons and daughters; as an opportunity provided by nature and well worth taking advantage of.

All of this kept me going in the one direction. Then one day I was speaking to a woman in a clothing boutique and mentioned my involvement with childbirth and the research I had conducted on third stage. She said, 'You would love to speak to a woman who is visiting from America'. She gave me the phone number of Clair Lotus Day, the initiator of Lotus Birth! I rang Clair and she was just about to leave to catch her plane home. I wouldn't be able to see her. She told me about Lotus Birth – the practice of leaving the baby 'whole' and allowing the cord and placenta to come away from the navel in its own time. A week later material arrived from America which gave accounts of these beautiful births.

Clair Day, a clairvoyant with the ability to see auras, could see the cord trauma damage in people's auras. In babies who didn't have that trauma she saw whole, strong vibrant auras. I think that our auras indicate the health, or otherwise, of our immune system. The information that has come to light while compiling this book not only supports Clair Day's position, but also *raises some very disturbing questions about what is being done to newborns and their mothers when the cord is cut immediately after birth*. This research is presented in the chapter 'Leaving well alone' by Dr Sarah Buckley, and it may well shock you.

Lotus Birth had been practised in America for 11 years. I began sharing the information with people via articles in newsletters and workshops and compiled a booklet from the material Clair had sent. People were very interested and many people started leaving their baby's cord attached for hours after the birth.

It wasn't until 1986 that Australia's first full Lotus Birth occurred. On the night of a full eclipse of the moon, the festival of Wesak (one of the high points of the esoteric calendar, the time when the ascended masters are closest to the earth) and the night Haley's comet left the southern skies, Kushna Warszewski gave birth to Tika, her fourth child, her third home birth, second water birth and first lotus-born baby.

It was a first for us all. Journeying over the next seven days was a passage into the unknown. Kushna had made a beautiful placenta bag during her pregnancy and she found it ideal for keeping Tika's wrapped placenta. All went well and on the seventh day Tika let go of her placenta and cord.

There have been hundreds of Lotus Births since. You'll read some of their stories in this book. It has been amazing how quickly the information moved. I've had enquiries from as far away as Italy!

I was teaching regularly in New Zealand at that time and the midwives there loved it. Parents all around Australia, particularly on the East Coast, in Western Australia, Tasmania and Alice Springs, where I hold Women's Mysteries five-day retreats, have embraced this beautifully profound birthing rite.

You will meet some of these parents in this book. I hope you enjoy their stories. They are joined by doctors, midwives, psychologists, philosophers and researchers in what, I hope, gives a full and rounded account of the influences that have brought this ancient birth rite of the pharaohs back into awareness, so that it can be available to new beings being born among us. This book is a product of community – of people coming together and sharing their lives.

Chapter 1

Womb ecology becomes world ecology

Shivam Rachana

These Lotus Birth babies are different. They are more whole – more like babies used to be. Today's babies are often very worried – they show signs of stress. This is concerning; that stress is increasing even in babies.

The most striking example of wellness I have seen in a lotus-born baby was a baby whose father had died during the pregnancy. When this happens one can expect that the child will manifest symptoms of distress related to the mother's emotional state. This lotus-born child was completely clear of the residual trauma that these cases usually carry. She was very calm and centred. From my observations of the babies I see in my practice I find Lotus Birth most beneficial. 🐚

Helma Bak, Dutch-born medical doctor practising anthroposophical medicine and homoeopathy in Australia.

THE spiritual relationship between child and parents is not a notion that finds discussion in our culture. However, other cultures, mainly indigenous, do acknowledge and tend this aspect of human life on earth. An example that I particularly like is from a culture I have heard about where a woman wanting a child spends time in nature. Through meditative practice she comes to know the sound of the baby who is to incarnate. She teaches this sound to her partner and when they make love, they make that sound. She teaches her midwives the sound and they use it during her labour. Whenever the baby is fitful or, in later life, unwell, that sound is used to soothe and heal. After the person dies the sound is never used again.

These people know about the interconnectedness of all beings. Just as we know that each individual has their own unique fingerprint, they know that we also have a signature sound. The understanding and use of sound for healing is well known among some peoples; the Tibetans probably being the most well-known of those.

Many indigenous cultures have a strong sense of being part of a continuum. Our isolated 'me' culture deprives us of this. If we reflect on how most of us were born – drugged, isolated from our mother and deprived of basic mammalian needs of access to the breast, skin-to-skin contact and holding – we might begin to understand more fully the difficulties we have in our interpersonal relationships.

The implications of Lotus Birth are best approached through the perspective of the ancient mystery traditions, developed in places as diverse as India, China and Egypt. Through disciplines of contemplation and meditation, these traditions have developed an understanding of the totality of a human being that is still absent from Western medical science. Generally, they articulate dimensions across which human beings live simultaneously, and how disharmony or trauma in one affects the others.

To fully understand the implications of Lotus Birth, it is help-ful to have an understanding of the five bodies, which, according to many Eastern teachings, comprise the totality of our being.

physical body
emotional body
mental body
etheric body
spiritual body

There are vital energies, which are part of all living things, that flow through and around our bodies. These energies, known as *auras,* can be seen by some people. Chinese systems of acupuncture describe how an energy, known as *chi,* flows along meridians throughout the body. It extends beyond the physical body (as we generally regard it) to form the auric field, or aura, around the body. This auric field is our interface with other dimensions of subtle energies. A strong auric field helps to preserve the integrity of the organism.

This understanding of the human being is ancient and world-wide, although not part of the general Western notion of reality. Quantum physics, however, is leading scientists to recognise these phenomena as valid.

In time, I am sure, we shall be able to prove that a strong auric field is indicative of a strong immune system. Holes or damage in the auric field manifest as a weak immune system. These damaged areas provide the energetic grid from which many degenerative diseases manifest.

From a wholistic perspective, the practice of Lotus Birth is most logical.

Lotus Birth slows things down. This is most desirable. The time after a birth is to be savoured. It is like the time after making love, after the climax, a time of intimacy and integration. A mother who has just birthed her baby, after nine months of pregnancy, benefits greatly from quiet and rest. The birth experience requires integration. Time to reflect on things and to be able to talk about it all with supportive people is most beneficial. The father and other children who may have been present also appreciate and benefit from this 'between times'.

Lotus Birth provides a unique opportunity after the birth for the family to settle in, to be together in a very special way. With the placenta still attached, the sense of being in the space 'between worlds' is very apparent. The baby is here but is still there. The time of transition from the beyond into the physical plane of existence is obvious. These first few days see the digestive tract and the elimination system, both of which are part of placental function, become established in the baby's body.

We may well wonder whether the hectic stress-filled lives many of us lead are a reflection of our very first hours and days in hospitals – hustle and bustle and the tyranny of time.

Taking time – 'being' in time – for the first days of life may well be the panacea for 80% of the diseases from which we suffer which are stress related.

To begin in a place away from positive ion-producing machines such as computers, televisions, mobile phones, microwave ovens and air conditioning allows the baby's systems and subtle bodies to align and the organism to find its own integrity. This is the point from which the baby will relate to itself and others. Breastfeeding establishes with greater ease in this environment.

The creation of the placenta is one of the most mysterious and ingenious acts of creation, one about which we actually know very little, even though our very existence has depended on it.

Six days after the sperm from our father merged with the ovum – which our mother had carried in her body since she, herself, was developing inside our grandmother – this tiny six-day old organism (us), about to attach itself to the uterine wall, undergoes a still not understood process that causes the same genetic material to go two ways. Some becomes the baby and some the placenta.

Alternatively, we could regard the baby and the placenta as a single unit – with the placenta an essential organ, such as the heart or liver, functioning and necessary for survival. However, we don't say, 'some of the genetic material turns into the baby and some turns into the heart or lungs', so why do we conceptually separate the placenta from the baby?

Lotus Birth establishes the baby–placenta relationship and suggests that the mother gives birth to the baby–placenta. As we shall see, there are no sustainable medical reasons for cutting the cord and separating the biological unit that conceived, grew and delivered (or birthed) together.

Current birthing practice is to cut the cord while the placenta is still in the mother. When this happens, people do not perceive the complete biological unit of baby–placenta and as a consequence find it difficult to imagine the biological-historical-genetic-foetal unity of the placenta–baby. As the practice continues, many mothers never even see their baby's placenta and some think that the placenta is theirs. Lotus Birth puts the placental ownership clearly with the baby, where it belongs.

The moment of the baby's 'letting go' of the umbilicus and placenta has its origin at the moment of implantation of the egg into the uterus. This moment of implantation heralded, in a most organic way, the beginning of another human life. Twenty-five per cent of conceptions do not reach this stage, because the uterus does not accept implantation of the egg.

Implantation is a two-way event. It is an acceptance by the mother's uterus of the new life form and a commitment by the fertilised ovum to go to the next stage of gestation. It is a key point in the mother–child relationship, and in a woman's relationship with her partner, to accept into her deep and sacred place the product of their union.

I have worked with some women who have conceived and not wanted to continue with the pregnancy. They have connected with their babies and negotiated a 'let go'. The baby has left. It is a very conscious act. It is negotiable. It is done through a process of connecting with the spirit being of the incoming child, and through an exploration and articulation of both conscious and unconscious aspects of the pregnancy.

Good birth preparation programs provide instruction and practices for parents to connect to their child in utero. The babies are very responsive and this connection is wonderful for the parents.

For the baby implantation is a major step in its commitment to incarnation. Embodiment will mean reliance on the ongoing supply of nutrients from the placenta via the umbilicus. This is now the foetus' life-line, on which he or she is dependent. The new being becomes open to receiving nourishment from this source.

At the earliest stages of development – just six days gestation – an estimated 30,000 different proteins have been identified in the embryonic human. The placenta is most complex, not the simple anchor for the cord or the passive sieve through which nutrients pass from mother to foetus, as many think. It has its own metabolism, which regulates maternal functions by producing hormones actively and selectively transferring substances between mother and baby and keeping equilibrium between the two, while keeping foetal and maternal blood circulation separate – *it is an organ of high intelligence.* Its function begins after implantation – that crucial point when, by forming burrowing projections, the baby attaches to the lining of the uterus.

This stage is a significant one. The mother's womb accepts the baby and the baby commits to the gestation. It is most intimate, most personal, and the disengagement at birth, nine months later, is connected to this point. It is a commitment and a release, and may have the most profound ramifications in the mother–

child relationship. Here is the organic foundation of this primal relationship.

The placenta establishes itself during the first ten weeks of pregnancy and by three months it is fully mature. It feeds nutrients to the baby via the umbilical cord and carries away and processes waste products. It provides a two-way exchange through the three large arteries of the umbilical cord.

There are sound physical reasons for not cutting the cord, which have to do with the blood value and volume that the baby would otherwise miss out on. The baby's emotional life and implications for its future relationships are further factors. Beyond that, there is the etheric level and the transference of energies.

Lotus Birth ensures that the physical body is well cared for by ensuring that the baby receives the full quotient of the oxygen-bearing highly nutritious blood that is in the cord. The infant obtains 40 to 60 mL of 'extra' blood from the placenta if the cord is not tied until pulsations cease. The loss of 30 mL of blood to the newborn is equivalent to the loss of 600 mL to an adult. Common practice of immediate cutting of the cord before the pulsations cease deprives the newborn of a possible 60 mL of blood, the equivalent of a 1200 mL haemorrhage in an adult. This is a likely explanation of the strange phenomenon of weight loss that most newborns seem to endure. The new organism is put immediately under undue stress to reproduce the blood it was denied.

We must wonder, too, whether the denial of the iron-rich cord blood is a contributing factor to widespread cases of infant and childhood anaemia.

The immature liver is supported by the placenta in the offloading of toxins, as the pumping action continues until the cessation of pulsations. Most babies' bodies are loaded up with these, including any drugs administered during the birth, and have to begin life dealing with the unnecessary toxic waste in their immature systems.

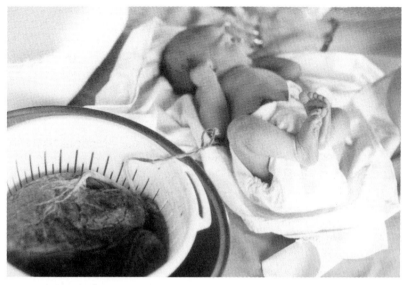

Draining the placenta   Photo: Simone Lukacs

The emotional body is nourished by a lack of stress on the new organism. It enjoys the ongoing support of the placenta, which allows the flow of oxytocin (the love hormone), as opposed to adrenaline, which is generated by the fear-or-survival (or fight-or-flight) mechanism.

This allows the baby the primal imprint of happiness and bliss as it takes in its first sights, sounds, smells and tastes.

Once the cord is emptied of blood we have a beautiful flat silvery ribbon; however, its function continues. Transference from the placenta is still occurring. Life force still in the placenta is transferred to the baby. This transference continues until the baby's auric field is complete. During this time, which can take three to seven days, the cord becomes brown and brittle. At the point of auric completion the cord simply comes away at the navel – the child is lotus born.

Protocol for a Lotus Birth
- Wait for the placenta to be born naturally. Place the Placenta in a bowl near the baby. It can stay there until you are ready to put it in a strainer. There is no hurry – 24 hours is okay.
- Wash the placenta gently in warm water, remove any blood clots and pat dry.
- Babies appear to like being told what is happening – even though we may think they don't yet understand.
- Wrap the placenta in absorbent material (a nappy or cloth), which is changed every day. Some people use salt to absorb the moisture. A placenta bag can be used.
- Ensure that the placenta is close to the baby so as not to cause any pulling on the cord.
- Lift the baby carefully for feeding and cuddles.
- Clothe the baby loosely; a nightgown with buttons on the front is good.
- When the cord becomes brittle take care. You can wet it to soften it and reshape it. It then dries again.
- Put the baby's nappies on loosely, and place extra nappies underneath the baby. These can be easily changed.
- This is a quiet still time – keep the space free of television and mobile phones.

Chapter 2

The story of childbirth

In this chapter we shall explore the psychohistory of childbirth practices in Western culture to give us a perspective of the role Lotus Birth plays in bringing back into balance the vital forces of the masculine and feminine.

We will consider forces that brought about the extraordinary imbalance that has rendered women passive participants in the most powerful moments of their lives, and steps that have helped revert this imbalance. Lotus Birth is one of those steps.

Birth in the masculine gaze

Deva Daricha

THE Second World War is a watershed for the rise of the modern military industrial state. As this aggressive form of social organisation has gradually gripped the consciousness of increasing numbers of planetary citizens, the mindset of this way of life has also infiltrated the general health system and, in particular, the practice of birth.

The modern materialistic scientific mind has exiled itself from Spirit and nature. The 'conquest of nature', which is the mission of this form of thought, has sought to abolish the natural mystery and to replace it with that which is known, knowable, predictable and safe. The mystery of incarnation, where Spirit descends into biological form and emerges as intelligence in carbon-based life form, has no place in a scientific laboratory filled with petri dishes, pipettes, eggs and sperm, donors, surrogates, pharmaceuticals and air conditioning.

The carnage of the First and Second World Wars impacted not only on all those who participated in them, but also impacted on the awareness of later populations in ways that we are still coming to understand. The rise of modern technological childbirth dates from the early 1950s. It was in these years that the doctors and nurses who had been in the front lines in the Second World War and were surrounded by so many medical emergencies in such catastrophic circumstances, were transformed in their awareness of birth from a natural process into a life-threatening situation.

Additionally, manufacturers of medical equipment, who had expanded rapidly during the war years, had to define new products and identify new markets for their *market share and profitability* to continue after the war years. It is not surprising that the major company involved in the production of genetically modified food seeds in our time was actually a major producer of toxic defoliants that devastated both landscape and human beings in Vietnam. This *war against nature*, this demand that nature give up its secrets, is the war of masculinised consciousness against the feminine energy. And birth is the realm where the feminine energy historically has been the strongest.

Another impact of the Second World War was the marshalling of huge numbers of women into the war effort. This was the first time that substantial numbers of women worked on assembly lines – those extraordinary, predictable, efficient, linear production devices. Prior to this time, apart from clerical work, retail assistants, teaching, librarianship and nursing, the vast majority of women were excluded from the paid workforce, but had their own domain of the feminine, the home, which was a site of production of goods for the family. The various clubs to which women belonged (church, school, sporting, community) provided a realm where masculine consciousness was not predominant. As increasing numbers of women entered the industrial processes of production, they entered into the realm of masculinised consciousness. We can surmise they generally accepted that this was how the world worked, so that as the impersonal efficient time-governed routines of industrial production came to control their lives in the productive realm, the same types of thinking and acting came to control their birthing in the re-productive realm. The baby-boom years of the 50s and 60s saw production-line obstetrics in action. As we reflect on the social changes we ourselves experienced in living through the last half of the twentieth century, we each can generate our own historical account of this masculinisation of the collective consciousness.

As the participation of women in the workforce increased and as it became obvious to them that they could do things as well as men in areas from which they had previously been excluded, the movement for equality gained momentum. However, what was overlooked initially was that this was a claim for *equal participation in a system designed and delineated by masculinised consciousness*. The lunar rhythms of a woman's organic and emotional life, the changing states of consciousness that can occur for a woman as a pregnancy advances, and the domestic needs of a mother and her children are all irrelevant and not important in such a system. Not only are the woman/mother's needs ignored, but also the *children's needs are ignored where masculinised consciousness is predominant*.

We also need to be mindful of the possibility that in the public domain where birth is taken away from the home, relatives, friends, and familiar surroundings, it may function as an arena of unconscious social conflict. We know from many different ethnic groups in our communities that women from different cultures, languages, religions, races and birthing practices receive scant concern in a situation where most people are treated without consideration for individual differences.

The enforced docility of birthing women has as its historical antecedent the teachings by Jay Marion Simms and others who had been travelling to wealthy homes in America to anaesthetise women for sexual intercourse, according to the belief that the more passive a woman, the more attractive she was to her husband and the closer to the state nature intended for *him*. Just as the workers in the early industrial factory processes were being reduced to cogs in a large functioning machine, so were the natural processes of the feminine being sedated into ways acceptable to masculinised consciousness.

The beginnings of the modern Western 'drug problem' can be traced back to approximately two decades after the substantial increase in the use of analgesia in childbirth. In such ways does the suppression of the feminine into the darkness come back to haunt us through our children.

If it was a nice day, a really nice day, I would like to be born under the stars.

RD Laing

The depersonalisation of birth

In his extraordinary chapter on the psychological aspects of childbirth in *The Psychology of Birth* (by Leslie Feher), Louis E Mehl systematically outlines the ways in which physicians in labour wards cope with anxiety: by splitting off from emotional relationship with the patient, and by depersonalising the birthing mother through standardised medical ritual procedures and clothing.

Mehl writes: 'Childbirth is of central importance in every culture. Every society has fertility rites, birth myths and art, and persons whose duties to the community involve attending births. Because birth is so necessary for the preservation of the society, childbirth practices tend to reflect the deepest values of the culture. This is true also for the other rites of passage, including the transition to adulthood, marriage and death, but birth has been more difficult to study anthropologically because it has usually been a private family-friend affair, whereas these other events tend to involve the entire community.'

Birth has become a technical rather than an emotional experience in the same way as death – both take place within a sterile hospital atmosphere. Emotions have become controlled by chemicals rather than being expressed in a healing environment. The intimacy and emotional power of childbirth can be stripped away by the impersonal attitudes of hospital staff and technical procedures they use. In the West this depersonalisation has been regarded as progressive; however, these ostensibly progressive changes have a profound cultural impact on individuals and families. Making birth and death technical rather than significant life events is symptomatic of a deeper process of technological control over our lives.

The technologisation of the twentieth century has contributed to a move away from the traditional childbirth practices – home birth attended by a midwife – to birth in hospital assisted by instruments and drugs. In this environment the baby is separated from the mother and both are isolated from the family. Instead they are surrounded by machines, routine, doctors, nurses, and an impersonal approach.

Obstetrics courses in medical schools ensure that the birth practices developed from the 1920s to the 1950s remain pervasive in the West. Allopathic medicine, which represents the medical model as we know it today, tends to ignore the psychological factors affecting health, as well as the traditional organic herbal remedies.

'This allopathic tradition involves reliance on drugs and surgery to relieve symptoms, rather than more holistic techniques aimed at preserving health, via good exercise and a healthy lifestyle. Giving birth under this regime is a very sterile undertaking, literally and figuratively,' according to Mehl. In the 50s, the woman came to the hospital early in labour. Once admitted, her pubic hair was shaved, she was given an enema, and often an intravenous solution. The course of birth was very lonely as her husband or support person was not allowed to be with her, not even in the labour room. During labour pain medication (such as meperidine (Pethidine), morphine, and Nysentil) was routinely administered. At the time of the pushing stage a general anaesthesia was given so the baby had to be delivered with forceps over a wide episiotomy. Mehl describes the alienating atmosphere of the labour room: 'During delivery the woman was flat on her back on a delivery table with sterile drapes over everything except her vagina and perineum. Everyone present would be garbed in caps, masks, sterile suits and sterile operating garb. There was little place for humanity. Doctors and nurses would chatter, as they do during surgery, about sports and politics, well spiced with sexual innuendos and sexual game playing between doctor and nurse. Once the patient was under general anaesthesia, she would not infrequently be the object of humour or ridicule. After the birth the baby would go to the nursery. The mother might not see her child for the first twenty-four hours, and thereafter only every four hours for feeding during the day.'

Birth controlled by technology

Mehl also points out the conditioned cultural helplessness of birthing women, which is perpetuated by attitudes towards hospital births. 'In routine technological delivery, it remains common for the woman to enter the hospital in very early labour – 2 cm cervical dilation – largely because she has never been adequately instructed about the feelings to expect. So she is put in bed and conditioned to a passive role, both physically and mentally. She spends hours lying around, as little happens to move labour along, whereas in fact walking and activity, and an active energised mind, are most useful for good labour to progress.' Passivity is a common cause of failure of the uterus to contract effectively. Hence it becomes necessary to administer the hormone oxytocin to encourage the contractions, with risks for mother and baby.

A passive mental attitude also increases pain sensation: by focusing on pain it becomes more intense. This then leads to more passivity. When hard labour finally begins, it is experienced more intense than it otherwise might.

Electronic foetal monitoring is common. To do this the amniotic sac (bag of waters) is ruptured, and a catheter pushed through the vagina and cervix past the foetus' head into the uterus to record the strength of uterine contractions. Then a metal electrode is applied to the baby's scalp to monitor the baby's heart rate.

Mehl also is critical of the drugs given routinely to birthing women: 'Pain relieving drugs are ordinarily given after 4 cm cervical dilation. Epidural anaesthesia may be given at 5 to 6 cm of cervical dilation. This is done by threading a catheter through a needle into the space around the dura (the covering of the spinal cord) in the low back area of the spine. The anaesthetic is infused through this catheter to bathe the nerves and cause numbness in the areas reached by them, including the abdomen and the lower legs. The ability to move is greatly diminished, and occasionally there is significant hypotension (low blood pressure) at the time of placement of the epidural. This can cause distress in the baby by decreasing the amount of blood (and therefore oxygen) received from the placenta. Spinal anaesthetics are similar to epidurals, but they involve more risk.'

Often the medical interference does not benefit the patient but the doctor or medical students: 'In some hospitals it is routine practice for all women having their first child to be given epidural anaesthesia and to have a forceps delivery. This can be simply because the resident physicians (registrars) want more training and experience in the use of forceps. The residents (registrars) and nurses encourage the woman to accept drugs and epidural anaesthesia by telling them how good it will feel to be free of the pain, and that it will not harm the baby in any way. This constitutes a powerful indirect hypnotic suggestion. After delivery the mother then feels she could not have given birth without the aid of forceps and medical intervention, not realising that the anaesthetia made her unable to push and therefore necessitated the use of forceps.'

The medicalisation of childbirth as a social tool teaches women a dependent, patient role. This process could be called indirect hypnosis. According to Mehl, it is 'a powerful means of convincing women who are in a naturally vulnerable state while in labour that unnecessary procedures are essential, so that they in turn become grateful to the physician-rescuer. The essence of such socialisation is the creation of a class of women willing to allow their births to be controlled by technology.' However, not only birth but also other natural transitions in a woman's life are thus medicalised: menstruation, family planning, menopause. 'In this way, women become socialised into being dependent upon physicians and the medical establishment to cope with their normal, natural physiological functions.'

There is now a growing movement to humanise childbirth – women demanding control over their own labour, the emotional support of their families rather than anaesthesia to deal with pain, and immediate contact with their babies. While not negating pain, Mehl advocates birth as a positive experience: 'At its most self-aware, the new consciousness accepts the painful aspect of parturition and assents that pleasure can exist parallel to pain, insisting on complete sentience and even finding childbearing a transcendental experience, ecstatic to the mother and, perhaps, also for the child. There is a growing concern with how to make the birth experience a source of profound personal growth for the mother and a psychologically/spiritually positive experience for the infant.'

The emergence of the gentle birth movement
Shivam Rachana

L ET'S take a brief look at the historical development of awareness around the birth process, so that we can place Lotus Birth as part of a continuum of development in Western thought regarding childbirth.

Generally, the outcome of birth is parallel to life expectancy. Improvements in nutrition and sanitation and the understanding of infection have had the most dramatic effect on what are now regarded as better outcomes for mother and child. Child mortality has decreased and life expectancy continues to grow.

Up to the 1940s, birth had been the realm of midwives, and most babies were born at home. With the Industrial Revolution thousands had moved to the cities to find employment. In the cramped city environments, much was changed from the community-oriented village existence. Women continued to become pregnant and babies were born; however, they were lacking the supportive environment experienced by previous generations.

Having babies traditionally is Women's Business in all indigenous cultures, and was so in Western culture up until that time. The people building and managing cities were men, and men were making decisions about things they didn't really understand. To enable doctors to care more efficiently for the ill, they built hospitals, gigantic buildings full of the sick and dying. Hospital also became the place to which a woman had to go when she was about to deliver her baby.

People working in hospitals have a certain way of looking at things that enables them to identify what's wrong with a person and how best to address the problem. This is appropriate when somebody presents with a problem. It is not a helpful attitude for a normal healthy birth.

Birth thus became regarded as a series of wrongs that had to be righted. The first lying-in hospitals were actually designed to give trainee doctors and obstetricians the chance to attend women in labour, and had very high mortality rates due to doctors' ignorance of sepsis. By the 1950s all women found themselves ritually shaved, laid on their backs, strapped into metal stirrups, cut open and anaesthetised, when all they wanted was to have a baby.

Modern birthing practices saw the mother arbitrarily drugged and the baby consequently delivered drugged and usually screaming or needing resuscitation. Large numbers of babies were dragged from their drugged mothers with forceps, their mothers never knowing details of the birth, or remembering much of it afterwards.

Brutally held upside down and hit on the bottom, the newborn was 'welcomed' into the world. This was followed by separation from the mother in a large room full of other babies, and by days of starvation, as the mother's colostrum (first milk) was considered 'useless'.

Most of us, if we were born in a hospital environment, were initiated into the world in this way. Today research on the brain patterns of sleeping babies – often regarded as 'good' babies – shows that they are like those of brains in shock.

Gradually women, who up to that point had seen doctors as the experts knowing more about birth than they themselves did, began to stir from their apathy and take initiative. The 1960s saw a grass roots revolution as women began to practise mental, emotional and physical birth preparation, known as psychoprophylaxis. They learnt to relax their bodies and consciously breathe through contractions while focusing their minds on a chosen focal point in the room.

Women delivering their babies free of drugs were talking about giving birth with joy and deep satisfaction. Fathers and friends made their way into the labour wards to support the birthing woman. Many and varied are the stories of how they were or were not received by hospital staff. Dr Lamaze in France and Dr Grantly Dick-Read in America became known for their support of this latest development in birthing practices.

Breastfeeding, which had fallen victim to the march of 'progress' via the multi-national formula companies, supported by the medical profession, began to return from its demise as women remembered the natural way of caring for their babies.

The next leap in our evolution was a return to a more gentle birth. In 1967, Dr Frederick Leboyer awoke the Western obstetrics world to the possibility that the baby was a feeling participator in the birth process. In his book and film *Birth without Violence*, Leboyer brought attention to the sensitivity of the newborn and the impact of birth practices on the development of the child. Leboyer suggested that the baby's screaming was indicative of distress, and that the conditions into which the new members of society were being received be examined in the light of what was good for the baby.

Leboyer highlighted the violent way in which the newborn was treated when delivered in a modern hospital environment. Leboyer himself had delivered thousands of babies in the orthodox way. It was only after experiencing his own birth in primal therapy that he awoke to the impact birthing practices had on the baby. That moment of birth, a time of openness to the new, a time of life-forming impressions, in his eyes was barbaric beyond belief.

Leboyer drew attention to the impact of drugs on the unborn child. The assault of cold air-conditioning on new, exposed skin, of bright lights on eyes opened for the first time, of clashing instruments and loud voices on ears used to the muffled sounds of underwater frequencies, of having the oxygen supply through the umbilicus severed before the supply of air to the lungs was fully established – all contributed to the trauma a newborn child experienced at birth.

'Birth without violence' was his cry for reform. Leboyer advocated no drugs for the mother; soft lighting and warm air in the delivery suite; and a gentle delivery which included careful massage and floating the newborn in a tub of warm water. Having re-experienced in therapy the pain of having his umbilical cord cut, Leboyer insisted on leaving the cord attached until it stopped pulsing, usually twenty or more minutes after delivery, arguing that the blood that fills it belongs in the baby's body. All who observed this method carried out were left in no doubt as to the beneficial impact on the newborn and the happy parents.

The Leboyer Method, as it became known, was welcomed by many parents who found supportive doctors to attend them.

However, it was derided by many who found it much more satisfying to cut cords, drug women, cut them open and hear the scream of the newborn. This they considered as 'normal'. Yet hospitals that provided Leboyer births found their bookings swell and knew they were on to a good thing. Some offered modified Leboyer births. Leboyer deliveries also thrived in the fertile home birth sector.

Birth centres began sprouting everywhere. Sheila Kitzinger in the UK with her writings and appearances around the world inspired the notion of 'woman centred birth'. In the 1980s *water birth entered the picture*. The Western world began to hear about Russian births, where the baby was actually born under water. Startling photographs, and then film, showed how it was done. By then, the Russian experience was twenty years old. Many people felt an immediate resonance with this way of giving birth. Women found relief from the contractions in the supportive milieu of warm water. Women labouring in water found that it helped them enormously to relax, and reports of pleasurable, even ecstatic births were being heard. Babies made their entry from the womb into the warm waters of spas, tubs and baths. This new phase showed us that the 'facts' we believed and were taught about the newborn were full of inaccuracies.

In France, Michel Odent was becoming renowned for natural, instinctive births, many under water. Those who had never attended one had plenty to say about what they hadn't experienced; however, Michel Odent became the champion of a woman's right to birth her baby naturally.

There was also what Janet Balaskas in the UK popularised as Active Birth – when a woman takes control of the positions she uses to birth her baby, and her caregivers adapt to her needs. This has been a powerful influence on birthing practices in more recent times.

During all of these developments, SHE was awakening: SHE, who inhabits and expresses through the female form, was claiming

HER own process. Women were listening to their bodies and their babies in utero, knowing how their babies wanted to be born. Lotus Birth is part of this awakening.

Lotus Birth is a call to pay attention to the natural physiological process. Its practice, through witnessing, restores faith in the natural order.

Lotus Birth extends the birth time into the sacred days that follow and enables baby, mother and father and all family members to pause, reflect and engage in nature's conduct. Lotus Birth is a call to return to the rhythms of nature, to witness the natural order and to the experience of not doing, just being.

The expulsion of the placenta was probably intended by Nature to be accompanied by the force of gravity, with the mother in the squatting position. Waiting for separation and descent of the placenta has been traditional teaching for midwives – but this cherished idea should be abandoned.

(Myles Textbook for Midwives)

Chapter 3

Leaving well alone

A natural approach to the third stage of labour

Dr Sarah Buckley

Modern birthing practices
- With the birth of the anterior shoulder, oxytocic drugs are administered via injection into the mother's thigh.
- While the rest of the body is still inside the mother and only the head is born, the baby is subjected to suction tubes in nose and mouth.
- If the baby's cord is around its neck – 25% occurrence – it is clamped and cut before the body is born. Otherwise, when the body is fully born, the cord is clamped and cut.
- If the placenta doesn't follow the baby out – which it usually does not – cord traction is applied, that is, the doctor or nurse pulls on the cord to try to dislodge the placenta.

THE medical approach to pregnancy and birth has become so ingrained in our culture that we have forgotten the way of birth of our ancestors: a way that has ensured our survival as a species for millennia. In the rush to supposedly protect mothers and babies from misfortune and death, modern Western obstetrics has neglected to pay its dues to the Goddess, to Mother Nature, whose complex and elegant systems of birth are interfered with on every level by this new approach, even as we admit our inability to understand or control these elemental forces.

Medical interference in pregnancy, labour and birth is well documented, and the negative sequellae are well researched. However, *medical management of the third stage of labour* – the time between the baby's birth and the emergence of the placenta – to my mind, *is more insidious.* At the time when Mother Nature prescribes awe and ecstasy, we have injections, examinations, and clamping and pulling on the cord. Instead of body heat and skin-to-skin contact, we have separation and wrapping. Where time should stand still for those eternal moments of first contact, as mother and baby fall deeply in love, we have haste to deliver the placenta and clean up for the next 'case'.

This 'management ' of the third stage, which has been taken even further in the last ten years with the rising popularity of 'active management of the third stage' (see below), has its own risks for mother and baby. While much of the activity is designed to reduce the risk of maternal bleeding, or postpartum haemorrhage (PPH), which is most certainly a serious event, it seems that *the medical approach to labour and birth actually leads to many of the problems* that active management is designed to address.

Active management also creates specific and potentially life-threatening problems for mother and baby. In particular, use of active management leads to a newborn baby being deprived of up to half of his or her expected blood volume. This extra blood, which is intended to perfuse the newly functioning lungs and other vital organs, is discarded along with the placenta when active management is used, with possible sequellae such as breathing difficulties and anaemia, especially in vulnerable babies.

Drugs used in active management have documented risks for the mother, including death, and we do not know the long-term effects of these drugs, which are given at a critical stage of brain development, for the baby.

Hormones in the third stage

As a mammalian species – that is, we have mammary glands that produce milk for our young – we share almost all features of labour and birth with our fellow mammals. We have in common the complex orchestration of labour hormones, produced deep within our 'mammalian' (or middle) brain, to aid us and ultimately ensure the survival of our offspring.

We are helped in birth by three major mammalian hormone systems, all of which play important roles in the third stage as well. The hormone oxytocin causes the uterine contractions that signal labour, as well as helping us to enact our instinctive mothering behaviours. *Endorphins, the body's natural opiates, produce an altered state of consciousness* and aid us in *transmuting pain*: and the fight-or-flight hormones adrenaline and noradrenaline (epinephrine and norepinephrine – also known as catecholamines or CAs) give us the burst of energy that we need to push our babies out in second stage.

During the third stage of labour, strong uterine contractions continue at regular intervals, under the continuing influence of oxytocin. The uterine muscle fibres shorten, or retract, with each contraction, leading to a gradual decrease in the size of the uterus, which helps to 'shear' the placenta away from its attachment site. Third stage is complete when the placenta is delivered.

For the new mother, the third stage is a time of reaping the rewards of her labour. Mother Nature provides peak levels of oxytocin, the hormone of love, and endorphins, hormones of pleasure for both mother and baby. Skin-to-skin contact and the baby's first attempts to breastfeed further augment maternal oxytocin levels, strengthening the uterine contractions that will help the placenta to separate, and the uterus to contract down. In this way, oxytocin acts to prevent haemorrhage, as well as to establish, in concert with the other hormones, the close bond that will ensure a mother's care and protection, and thus her baby's survival.

At this time, the high adrenaline levels of second stage, which have kept mother and baby wide-eyed and alert at first contact, will be falling, and a very warm atmosphere is necessary to counter-act the cold, shivering feelings that a woman has as her adrenaline levels drop. If the environment is not well heated, and/or the mother is worried or distracted, continuing high levels of adren-aline will counteract oxytocin's beneficial effects on her uterus, thereby increasing the risk of haemorrhage (Odent 1992).

For the baby, too, the reduction in fight-or-flight hormones, which have also peaked at birth, is critical. If, because of extended separation, these hormones are not soothed by contact with the mother, the baby can go into psychological shock which, according to author Joseph Chilton Pearce, will prevent the activation of spe-cific brain functions that is nature's blueprint for this time. Pearce believes that the *separation of mother and baby after birth is 'the most devastating event of life, which leaves us emotionally and psychologi-cally crippled'* (Pearce 1992).

One might wonder whether the modern epidemic of 'stress' – the term was invented by researchers in the early twentieth cen-tury – and *stress-related illness in our culture is a further outcome of current third-stage practices*. It is scientifically plausible that our entire hypothalamic–pituatary–adrenal (HPA) axis, which medi-ates long-term stress responses and immune function, as well as short-term fight-or-flight reaction, is permanently mis-set by the continuing high stress hormone levels that ensue when newborn babies are routinely separated from their mothers.

Michel Odent, in his review of research on the 'primal period' (the time between conception and the first birthday), concludes that interference or dysfunction at this time affects the development of our 'capacity to love', which is particularly vulnerable around the time of birth, being connected hormonally to the oxytocin system (Odent 1998). Research by Jacobsen (1990, 1997) and Raine (1994), among others, suggests that contemporary tragedies such as *suicide, drug addiction and violent criminality may be linked to problems in the perinatal period* such as exposure to drugs, birth complications and separation from or rejection by the mother.

A crucial role for birth attendants in these times is to ensure that a woman's *mammalian instincts are protected and valued during pregnancy, birth and afterwards.* Ensuring unhurried and uninterrupted contact between mother and baby after birth, adjusting the temperature to accommodate a shivering mother, allowing skin-to-skin contact and breastfeeding, and not removing the baby for any reason – these practices are sensible, intuitive and safe, and help to synchronise our hormonal systems with our genetic blueprint, giving maximum success and pleasure for both partners in the critical function of child-rearing.

The baby, the cord, and active management

Adaptation to life outside the womb is the major physiological task for the baby in third stage. In utero, the wondrous placenta fulfils the functions of lungs, kidney, gut and liver for our babies. Blood flow to these organs is minimal until the baby takes a first breath, at which time huge changes begin in the organisation of the circulatory system.

Within the baby's body, blood becomes, over several minutes, diverted away from the umbilical cord and placenta and, as the lungs fill with air, blood is sucked into the pulmonary (lung)

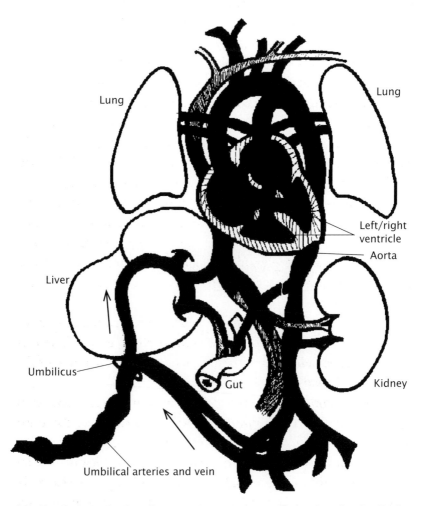

Lung

Lung

Left/right
ventricle

Aorta

Liver

Umbilicus

Gut

Kidney

Umbilical arteries and vein

Blood supply to the foetal organs   Illustration: Carolyn Tucker

While the baby is in utero the blood supply to the lungs, liver and gut is diverted
or reduced. The functions of these organs are performed by the placenta. With
the baby's first breath the diverting blood vessels close, causing the organs to
become fully perfused with blood for the first time.

The umbilical cord comprises three blood vessels – two umbilical arteries
that carry de-oxygenated blood to the placenta and a single umbilical vein that
returns oxygen-rich blood to the baby's body.

circulation. Mother Nature ensures a reservoir of *blood in the cord* and placenta that provides the additional blood *necessary for these newly perfused pulmonary and organ systems.*

The transfer of this reservoir of blood from the placenta to the baby happens in a step-wise progression, with blood entering the baby with each third-stage contraction, and some blood returning to the placenta between contractions. Crying slows the intake of blood, which is also controlled by constriction of the vessels within the cord (Gunther 1957) – both of which imply that the baby may be able to regulate the transfusion according to individual need.

Gravity will affect the transfer of blood, with optimal transfer occurring when the baby remains at or below the level of the uterus until the cessation of cord pulsation signals that the transfer is complete. This process of 'physiological clamping' typically takes three minutes, but may be longer, or can be complete in only one minute (Linderkamp 1982).

This elegant and time-tested system, which ensures that an optimum, but not a standard, amount of blood is transferred, is rendered inoperable by the current practice of early clamping of the cord – usually within 30 seconds of birth.

Early clamping has been widely adopted in Western obstetrics as part of the package known as active management of the third stage. This comprises the use of an oxytocic agent – a drug that, like oxytocin, causes the uterus to contract strongly – given usually by injection into the mother's thigh as the baby is born, as well as early cord clamping, and 'controlled cord traction' – that is, pulling on the cord to deliver the placenta as quickly as possible.

Haste becomes necessary, because the oxytocic injection will, within a few minutes, cause very strong uterine contractions that can trap an undelivered placenta, making an operation and 'manual removal' necessary. Furthermore, if the cord is not clamped before the oxytocic effect commences, the baby is at risk of having too much blood suddenly pumped from the placenta by the over-zealous contractions.

While the aim of active management is to reduce the risk of haemorrhage for the mother, 'its widespread acceptance was not preceded by studies evaluating the effects of depriving neonates [newborn babies] of a significant volume of blood' (Piscane 1996).

It is estimated that early clamping deprives the baby of 54 to 160 mL of blood (Usher 1963), which represents up to half of a baby's total blood volume at birth. '*Clamping the cord before the infant's first breath results in blood being sacrificed from other organs* to establish pulmonary perfusion [blood supply to the lungs]. *Fatality may result* if the child is already hypovolemic [low in blood volume]' (Morley 1997).

Where the baby is lifted above the uterus before clamping – for example during Caesarean surgery – blood will drain back to the placenta by gravity, making these babies especially liable to receive less than their expected blood volume. The consequence of this may be an *increased risk of respiratory* (breathing) *distress* – several studies have shown this condition, which is common in Caesarean-born babies, to be eliminated when a full placental transfusion was allowed (Peltonen 1981, Landau 1953).

The baby whose cord is clamped early also loses the iron contained within that blood – early clamping has been linked with an *extra risk of anaemia in infancy* (Grajeda 1997, Michaelson 1995).

These sequellae of early clamping were recognised as far back as 1801, when Erasmus Darwin wrote: 'Another thing very injurious to the child is the tying and cutting of the navel string too soon; which should always be left till the child has not only repeatedly breathed but till all pulsation in the cord ceases. As otherwise the child is much weaker than it ought to be, a part of the blood being left in the placenta which ought to have been in the child'.

In one study, premature babies experiencing delayed cord clamping – even only 30 seconds – showed a reduced need for transfusion, less severe breathing problems, better oxygen levels, and indications of probable improved long-term outcomes, compared to those whose cords were clamped immediately (Kinmond 1993).

Some studies have shown an increased risk of polycythemia (more red blood cells in the blood) and jaundice when the cord is clamped later. Polycythemia may be beneficial, in that more red cells means more oxygen being delivered to the tissues. The risk that polycythemia will cause the blood to become too thick (hyperviscosity syndrome), which is often used as an argument against delayed cord clamping, seems to be negligible in healthy babies (Morley 1998).

Jaundice is almost certain when a baby gets his or her full quota of blood, and is caused by the breakdown of the normal excess of blood to produce bilirubin, the pigment that causes the yellow appearance of a jaundiced baby. There is, however, no evidence of adverse effects from this (Morley 1998). One author has proposed that jaundice, which is present in almost all human infants to some extent, and which is often prolonged by breastfeeding, may actually be beneficial because of the anti-oxidant properties of bilirubin (Gartner 1998).

Early cord clamping carries the further disadvantage of depriving the baby of the oxygen-rich placental blood that mother nature provides to tide the baby over until breathing is well established. In situations of extreme distress – for example, if the baby takes several minutes to breathe – this reservoir of oxygenated blood can be life saving, but, ironically, standard practice is to cut the cord immediately if resuscitation is needed.

The placental circulation acts, when the cord is intact, as a conduit for any drug given to the mother, whether during pregnancy, labour or third stage. Garrison (1999) reports that Narcan, which is sometimes needed by the baby to counteract the sedating effect of pain-relieving drugs such as pethidine (demorol), given to the mother in labour, can be effectively administered via the mother's veins in third stage, waking the newborn baby in a matter of seconds.

The recent discovery of the *amazing properties of cord blood*, in particular the stem cells contained within it, heightens, for me, the need to ensure *that a newborn baby gets its full quota*. These cells are unique to this stage of development, and will migrate to the baby's bone marrow soon after birth, transforming themselves into various types of blood-making cells.

Cord blood harvesting, which is currently being promoted to fill cord blood banks for future treatment of children with leukaemia, involves immediate clamping, and up to 100 mL of this extraordinary blood can be taken from the baby to whom it belongs. Perhaps this is justifiable where active management is practised, and the blood would be otherwise discarded, but, unfortunately, cord blood donation is incompatible with a physiological (natural) third stage.

Active management and the mother

Active management (oxytocic, early clamping and controlled cord traction) represents a further development in third stage interference that began in the mid-seventeenth century, when male attendants began confining women to bed, and cord clamping was introduced to spare the bed linen.

Pulling on the cord was first recommended by Mauriceau in 1673, who feared that the uterus might close before the placenta was spontaneously delivered (Inch 1984). In fact, the recumbent (lying) postures, increasingly adopted under doctors' care, meant that spontaneous delivery of the placenta was less likely: the upright postures that women and midwives have traditionally used encourage the placenta to fall out with the help of gravity.

The first oxytocic to be used medically was ergot, derived from a fungal infection of rye. Ergot was known to to be used by seventeenth and eighteenth century European midwives. Its use was limited, however, by its toxicity. It was refined and revived in the 1930s, and by the late 1940s, some doctors were using it preventatively, as well as therapeutically, for postpartum haemorrhage (Inch 1984). Potential side effects from ergot derivatives include a rise in blood pressure, nausea, vomiting, headache, palpitations, cerebral haemorrhage, cardiac arrest, convulsion and even death.

Synthetic oxytocin, which mimics the effects of natural oxytocin on the uterus, was first marketed in the 1950s, and has largely replaced ergot derivatives, although a combination drug, called ergotamine, is still used, especially for severe haemorrhage. Syntocinon causes an increase in the strength of contractions, whereas ergot causes a large, 'tonic' contraction, which also increases the chance of trapping the placenta. Ergot also interferes with the process of placental separation, increasing the chance of partial separation (Sorbe 1978).

Recently active management has been proclaimed 'the routine management of choice for women expecting a single baby by vaginal delivery in a maternity hospital' (Prendville 1999), mostly because of the results of the recent Hinchingbrooke trial, comparing active versus 'expectant' (physiological) management.

In this trial (Rogers 1998), which involved only women at low risk of bleeding, active management was associated with a postpartum haemorrhage (blood loss > 500 mL) rate of 6.8%, compared with 16.5% for expectant (non-active) management. Rates of severe PPH (loss > 1,000 mL) were low in both groups – 1.7% active and 2.6% expectant.

The authors note further that, from these figures ten women would need to receive active management to prevent one PPH. They add 'Some women . . . may rate a small personal risk of PPH of little importance compared with intervention in an otherwise straightforward labour, whereas others may wish to take all measures to reduce the risk of PPH'.

Reading this paper, one must wonder how it is that almost one in six women bled after 'physiological' management, and whether one or more components of Western obstetric practices might not be actually increasing the rate of haemorrhage.

Botha (1968) attended over 26,000 Bantu women over 10 years, and reports that 'a retained placenta was seldom seen . . . blood transfusion for postpartum haemorrhage was never necessary'. Bantu women deliver both baby and placenta while squatting, and the cord is not attended to until the placenta delivers itself by gravity.

There is some evidence that the practice of clamping the cord, which is not practised by indigenous cultures, contributes to both PPH and retained placenta by trapping extra blood (around 100 mL, as described above) within the placenta. This increases placental bulk, which the uterus cannot contract efficiently against, and which is more difficult to expel (Walsh 1968).

Other Western practices that may contribute to PPH include the use of oxytocin for induction and augmentation (speeding up labour) (Brinsden 1978, McKenzie 1979), episiotomy or perineal trauma, forceps delivery, Caesarean and previous Caesarean (because of placental problems – see Hemminki 1996).

Gilbert (1987) notes that PPH rates in her UK hospital more than doubled from 5% in 1969–70 to 11% in 1983–5, and she concludes, 'The changes in labour ward practice over the last 20 years have resulted in the re-emergence of PPH as a significant problem'. In particular, she links an increased risk of bleeding with induction using oxytocin, forceps delivery, long first and second stages (but not prolonged pushing) and the use of epidurals, which increase the chance of forceps and of a long second stage.

As noted, Western practices do not facilitate the production of a mother's own oxytocin, neither is attention paid to reducing adrenaline levels in the minutes after birth, both of which are physiologically likely to improve uterine contractions and therefore reduce haemorrhage.

Clamping the cord, especially at an early stage, may also cause the extra blood trapped within the placenta to be forced back through the placenta into the mother's blood supply with the third stage contractions (Doolittle 1966, Lapido 1971). This 'foeto-maternal transfusion' increases the chance of future blood group incompatibility problems, which occur when the current baby's blood enters the mother's blood stream, causing an immune reaction which can be reactivated and destroy the baby's blood cells in a subsequent pregnancy, causing anaemia or even death.

The use of oxytocin, which strengthens contractions, either during labour, or in third stage, has also been linked to an increased risk of foeto-maternal hemorrhage and blood group incompatibility problems (Beer 1969, Weinstein 1971).

The World Health Organization, in its 1996 publication *Care in Normal Birth: a practical guide*, argues that 'In a healthy population (as is the case in most developed countries), postpartum blood loss up to 1,000 mL may be considered as physiological and does not necessitate treatment other than oxytocics'. In relation to routine oxytocics and controlled cord traction, WHO cautions that 'Recommendation of such a policy would imply that the benefits of such management would offset and even exceed the risks, including potentially rare but serious risks that might become manifest in the future'.

Choosing a natural third stage

Choosing to forego preventative oxytocics, to clamp late (if at all), and to deliver the placenta by our own effort all require forethought, commitment, and choosing birth attendants who are comfortable and experienced with these choices.

A natural third stage is more than this, however – we must ensure respect for the emotional and hormonal processes of both mother and baby, remembering how unique this time is. Michel Odent stresses the importance of not interrupting, even with words, and believes that ideally the new mother feels unobserved and uninhibited in the first encounter with her baby (Odent 1992). This level of non-interference is uncommon, even in home and birth centre settings.

Lotus Birth, the subject of this book, gives us a further chance to 'slow the fire drill' after birth, as midwife Gloria Lemay puts it, and allows our babies the full metaphysical, as well as physical, benefit of prolonged contact with the placenta. Lotus Birth, like a good midwife, also secludes mother and baby in the early hours and days, ensuring rest and keeping visitors to a minimum.

Third stage represents a first meeting, creating a powerful imprint upon the relationship between mother and baby. When both are undrugged and quiet, fully present and alert, new potentials are invoked, and we discover more about ourselves, and the sacred origins of our capacity to love.

Disadvantages and effects of current practices

· Lack of time to establish air breathing (i.e. to transfer from cord-delivered oxygen to lung breathing) results in trauma.

· Routine sucking out of airways strips protective lining for the reception of air; sets up conditions for asthma/ allergies; baby deprived of experience of establishing its own breathing regime; contributes to diminished sense of self-confidence.

· Air-conditioned air for first breath: disconnects the baby from its organic reality – planet earth.

· Disorientation

· Loss of nourishment: the cord carries blood that is 30–50% of the baby's total blood supply. It is high in iron and oxygen.

· Lack of support by the cord–placenta waste disposal system highly compromises immature systems, e.g. liver, kidneys.

· Postpartum haemorrhage: the clamping of the cord before it has emptied itself of blood sets up an implosion on the maternal site, and an effective rupture occurs on the uterine wall.

· Blood banks: recent recognition of the value of cord blood and its healing properties has led to the establish- ment of 'cord blood banks' for use in the treatment of childhood leukaemia. It is pertinent to ask that if cord blood is so valuable, what does it mean for the newborn child to be deprived of it?

· One may well ask whether the routine deprivation of this vital blood from the newborn is a contributing factor to childhood diseases such as leukaemia and other forms of cancer.

Chapter 4

The placenta and cord in other cultures

Anand Khushi

Although we do not know of any indigenous cultures who have practised Lotus Birth, many traditional peoples hold the placenta in high esteem. Maori people bury the placenta ritually on the ancestral marae; the hmong, a hill tribe from South East Asia, believe that the placenta must be retrieved by the soul after death to ensure physical integrity in the next life: a hmong baby's placenta is buried inside the house of its birth. Monkey mothers carry the placenta with the baby until separation.

Dr Sarah Buckley, *Pregnancy* magazine, Spring 1998

'WHEN my daughter was born, I had gone into hospital for an induction, but decided in the middle of the night, when a full moon was shining, that I would shortcut the induction. I would commune with her, and she would be born. Half-an-hour later, much to my alarm, I had three enormous contractions and out came a baby, a blue-red slippery, slithering baby between my legs and a blue-red slippery, slithering cord. And it was the cord which fascinated me almost more than the baby. In my state of euphoria, exhaustion and fright, I had imagined it would look quite different. Like a neat, grey, silken thread, or a scarlet ribbon, or even post office string . . . all would have served quite well, but not this pulsating, fibrous, bloody bundle. I had no scissors, no knife. Oh God, I thought, my teeth.

'At this point, a nurse came scurrying, took one look at me and said "Oh, my God, doctor will be very cross".

'What she did with the cord I have no idea. I had turned my attention to the baby. But in some earlier civilisations, the cord would have been kept and buried as a magical link with the new soul. Swahili people interred the cord under the hut where the child had been born. They believed it would act like a homing beacon. The Maya buried the cords of male babies in battlefields, so that they would grow up as valiant fighters. Incas used the umbilical cord as a dummy for sick children, thinking it contained a cure. The cord was never to be thrown into the sea or a fire, as this might precipitate death from drowning or from burns. Each civilisation had its own set of beliefs but included a universal acceptance that the cord had magical properties, and that no man or woman could ever sever contact with that early lifeline. Why would you want to when it is the very stuff of our existence?' (Deveson).

In our Western techno-medical culture the cord and placenta are regarded as 'dirty waste'. The placenta is meticulously weighed, measured, assessed, and the results recorded, before it is thrown into an incinerator or hospital mulcher and annihilated soon after birth. In fact, in many hospitals it still is routine for the cord to be cut so soon after birth that the baby loses a third of its blood supply, which continues to pulse in cord and placenta for a time. A common problem is that the mother then goes into shock and retains the placenta in utero, thus triggering further intervention.

We must look to other cultures and their customs in order to understand our own sense of discomfort about the dismissive way in which placenta and cord are treated in our culture, and which we have come to regard as 'normal'.

If we examine ancient civilisations, we find a variety of beliefs.

'In Egypt, the pharaoh led processions preceded by his actual placenta, fixed to the top of a long pole with a dangling umbilical cord. Placental symbols since antiquity have been seen on temples, seals and shields and in cave paintings. Either tree-like or snake-like qualities may be emphasised' (Noble).

The placenta hieroglyphic was used in many words relating to a variety of feelings, situations and relationships which reflect the original physical role the placenta played in life for each human on this planet.

The Ora Hayim of the Shulhan Arukh (Code of Jewish Law) refers to the ancient practice of preservation and internment of the placenta to help keep the newborn warm. John Aubrey in *Remaines of Gentilism and Judaism* (1686–88) refers to the use of the placenta for purposes of divination.

When the European (and also African and South American) healers and midwives were branded as witches and murdered during the 500 years of persecution through the Inquisition, much information about traditional approaches to natural and wholistic childbirth was lost, including practices surrounding care of the placenta.

In some pockets of Europe, traditional practices, or the memories of these practices, lived on in storytelling and folklore.

Sometimes these memories of old customs find their echo in contemporary literature. Kerstin Ekman in her novel *Blackwater* relates that in the olden days in Sweden, people used to bury the placenta so that the earth would become as fertile as the woman who had given birth. In many cultures, the placenta was regarded as sacred. Giving the placenta back to the earth can hence be regarded as a sacrifice in the original sense: to give something sacred (Latin: *sacrum facere*).

In Kalotaszeg, Transylvania, the placenta was used in contraception. If a couple wanted no more children, they would burn the placenta of the last child and mix its ashes with water for the husband to drink.

The midwife in Hungary wiped the mother's face three times with the placenta before the mother bit the placenta (thereby preventing haemorrhage by ingesting the oxytocin of the placenta) and drank a glass of spiced wine.

The Kwakiutl Indians of British Columbia customarily buried the placenta of baby girls at the high water mark, believing this would make them expert at digging for clams. Males' placentas were left exposed for ravens to devour, enabling the boy to acquire prophetic vision.

The placenta has been used for healing also by the Chinese. A homoeopathic remedy is made from a baby's dried placenta and given to that person throughout their life as a tonic in case of anaemia, general weakness or neurasthenia.

Barren women in Chinese provinces would sometimes eat a placenta in an effort to cause pregnancy. The placenta was also said to obliterate birthmarks if rubbed on the disfigured area.

In Japan, during the tenth century, Yasuyori Sukune Tanba, a physician and author of the 30-volume *Inshirokata*, sometimes called the 'Ishinpo' ('Medical Instruction') emphasised that the washed and purified placenta should be buried because it was an integral part of the body and linked with the child's destiny. Like the Koreans, the Japanese often used decorative earthenware pots as placenta caskets. Those who were too poor for caskets would wrap the placenta in rice straw before burying it or throwing it in the river.

The Japanese formal burial ceremony began with washing the placenta in water, then sake. It was then wrapped in a blue or red silk cloth and placed in a wooden box ornamented with good luck emblems. The box was sealed with special mud and suspended in the north-west corner of the house for one day before being given to the midwife for burial. Some boxes also contained necessities to ensure a successful life. For a boy these might include writing brushes and an inkpad to encourage him to become a philosopher. Needle and thread might be placed in the boxes of girls to encourage them to become skilful in needlecraft.

Placental burial in Japan became even more formal in later times and took place in a special cemetery. It was customary for barren women to borrow the under-robe of a pregnant friend to wear while stepping across the buried placenta of a newborn, to invoke the blessing of fertility.

Until the nineteenth century, placentas might be buried at the entrances to Japanese homes. Sometimes this was done by an old man who had cut the cord and thereafter functioned as the child's godfather – his age invoking a long and prosperous life for the child.

It was once widely believed that body parts remained in sympathetic union with the person even after the physical connection was severed, so it followed that actions upon the placenta, which had formed part of someone, could have a powerful influence upon that person.

In Buddhist countries it is believed that an incomplete body is banned from the Kingdom of the Dead, so if the placenta is lost or destroyed, some element of both mother and child is lost to immortality. As a result, Buddhists who birth elsewhere, take the placenta home for burial in a favourite spot in the garden.

In Malaysia, the child and placenta are considered to be siblings and since it is believed that the two are reunited in death, the *kampong bidan* (midwife) carefully washes the placenta, cord and membrane and wraps them in a white cloth to be buried.

On the West coast of Sumatra, at Mandeling, the placenta was washed and either buried under the house or put in an earthenware pot, which was sealed and thrown into the river. This was practised to avert any unfavourable influence of the placenta upon the child.

The New Zealand Maoris also respect the placenta, which is buried in a special place on the ancestral marae in a ceremony followed by a time of ritual cleansing. Maori people know where their placenta is as their point of connection with the earth from which they sprang and to which they return.

The Hmong believe that after death, the dead person must collect the placenta, which is traditionally buried under the supporting post of the house, if the child is a boy.

Between New Guinea and Sulawesi, in the Babar archipelago, the placenta was mixed with ashes and placed in a small basket. Seven women, each armed with a sword, then accompanied it to a Citrus *hystryx* tree, from which it was hung. The swords frightened away any evil spirits, which might make the child ill if they captured its placenta.

On the islands of Saparoea, Haroekoe and Noessa Laut, in the Banda Sea, the placenta was sometimes buried at sea. First it was placed in an earthenware pot and covered with white cotton material. A hole in the pot ensured it would sink. The man in charge of the canoe was ordered to steer a straight course lest the child grow up aimless; the person who dropped the pot in the sea was told to look straight ahead so the child would grow up without a squint.

Some Australian Aborigines have a ceremony around the cord and placenta. At the time of cord cutting, the ancestors' spirits are acknowledged and the placenta is buried in the place where the child was born. The cord is twisted into a necklace and placed around the newborn's throat. This symbolises a spiritual connection that will enable the child to learn the language of the sacred knowledge that reaches back like a spiralling cord to the great Ancestors and the beginning of time,' Robert Lawlor records in *Voices of the First Day.*

All of these cultural traditions are underpinned by a belief in the existence of spirit or soul that inhabits the physical body. Thus the respectful care of the placenta has spiritual significance. It is an honouring of the tree of life, which has connected the baby to its mother throughout nine months of pregnancy, and has been the child's bridge from the celestial to the earthly realm. 'In primitive tribes the placenta was often called the "double", "soul", "secret helper", or "brother", and either was buried or placed in a tree or on top of a pole', writes Elizabeth Noble.

In respecting the placenta, we respect our origin and our connection to the beyond as the inspiration for our spirit, and to the earth as the nurturer of our body.

Perhaps the loving ritual practices that have existed for thousands of years do assist the soul of the incoming child to anchor in its physical body. In fact, it would be arrogant to think that there has been no purpose to these rituals, which have been practised for so long and with such consistency in so many cultures on earth.

The early severing of the cord and the rapid, impersonal disposal of the placenta in the modern hospital environment produce a different psychological imprint in the child: that its resources have been stolen and it is left alone, to its own devices. (These early experiences often surface later in adult therapy, particularly in rebirthing.) Communication channels that have existed for nine months are suddenly severed, without choice or adequate grieving time. Especially if the child is then separated from the mother, as is common in hospitals, fear looms large that mother is gone, that her love is no longer there. The child is thrown into a desperate struggle to survive: it must breathe or die, whether its lungs are ready or not.

Panic ensues. That, more often than not, is our first imprint of life on earth in the Western cultural framework. Is it a wonder then that Western culture is materialistic, devoid of spirit, and individualistic to the point of pathology? Mothers agonising over the process of separation of their adolescent children really relive the sense of separation they and their newborns experienced at birth.

'Is there ever complete release? Can we look forward to a time when we only need once a year to gloat over the memorabilia? Perhaps our fiercely independent children, coached by our individualistic culture, ease the separation. Western children do not seem to keep the connection pulsing in the way of their Japanese counterparts, who treasure a piece of the umbilical cord in a box. If we have truly grown up in the process of parenting, I would like to believe that we reach a magical age when we shed our obsessions like an unwanted skin' (Kroll).

Most people cannot shed their obsessions until they heal the rage, pain, fear and grief around the loss of their placenta (and the umbilical cord), and claim their right to be treated with gentleness, love, care and respect from the moment of birth. A desperate perceived need to survive drives this culture, even though in fact it consumes 85% of the entire resources of the planet.

Compared to the practices of so many of the world's cultures, current Western practice of early cutting of the cord and disposal of the placenta with the hospital's sterile trash is abnormal. The violence and disrespect with which the baby and mother are treated in the hospital environment are a direct result of the absence of the original custodians of care for women and babies – traditional midwives, who support, advocate and care for mother and babe in ways alien to our materialistic culture. These traditional ways of care have advantages over our modern technological efficiency that we have not even begun to contemplate.

Chapter 5

Lotus Birth and the psyche

Primary imprints and life patterns

Soni Stecker

Ready or not

CUTTING the cord is a metaphor for releasing a child when it is ready to move away from the protective parental environment. In the eponymous book, Debra Adelaide has collected a number of stories which speak eloquently of the need to let go, to view the child as an individual in his or her own right, a person who will encounter life on its own terms when the time comes. It is the parents' task then to not hold on to the bond longer than needed, and to give the child the necessary skills so he or she can act independently.

But what happens when the metaphorical cord is cut prematurely, before the child is ready? Some young adults are not ready to 'leave the nest' when their parents are ready for them to leave. This reluctance to let go of the metaphorical umbilical cord signifies a reluctance to leave the primary connection to security and sustenance. If young adults have a need to postpone the separation phase, what needs might babies have to not be separated at birth?

Birth trauma

The notion that birth trauma is associated with difficulties in later life is not new. Freud postulated that all neuroses are based on birth trauma, but did not think it could be accessed. Rank diverged from Freud in believing that the birth trauma could be resolved. Reich understood energies in the body and was the forerunner for bodytherapies to help patients access birth. Primal therapy founder Janov focuses on the separation trauma that many of his patients relived in therapy, and relates this to later problems with aloneness: 'If ever there was a key trauma with lifelong consequences it is the separation of the newborn from its mother right after birth. As if the long birth struggle had not been enough; as if the harsh delivery room conditions had not been enough – the infant is then actually taken away from the one person who has been its entire source of comfort, its entire world. No wonder so many neurotics cannot be alone: their initial entry into this world was marked by that catastrophic aloneness just after birth, when they were placed in a container, alone and uncomforted. If anything, the newborn needs to be held, comforted and touched more now than any other time in his life.'

Rough 'professional' handling by hospital personnel adds to the traumatic experiences that lead to separation anxiety. Often the placenta and umbilical cord feature in birth recall: patients 'have felt a burning sensation around the umbilicus during Primals, yet had no idea what the sensation meant. There evidently is a trauma about the premature cutting of the umbilical cord. This premature action affects the amount of oxygen in the system and the infant patient feels that cut-off before being ready to breathe independently.' Janov believes that cutting the umbilical cord too early makes the first experience of breathing traumatic instead of smooth. He postulates that Leboyer's methods of not cutting the cord until minutes after the birth make the first breath of air less painful. Leboyer felt that how we breathe at birth determines how we will breathe for the rest of our life.

In contrast with birthing procedures of conventional hospitals, Leboyer's methods allow the baby a 'continuity from womb to belly', being put on the mother's belly directly after birth. Leboyer babies are healthier and different from other babies in that they rarely cry and are bright and alert, curious and alive from early on.

Although their discoveries stemmed from the observation of different states – in Janov's case birth Primals and in Leboyer's birth itself – Janov and Leboyer arrived at similar conclusions: both internal and external factors before and during the birth experience lead to birth imprints. Moreover, the trauma of birth has lifelong effects on our behaviour, wellbeing and personality development.

Birth in the technological age

Babies enter life 'through man-made portals of pain', according to David Chamberlain. 'Ironically, since the majority of births moved from home to hospital . . . in the 1940s, normal babies born at term have been introduced to a new kind of pain: routine, medically-inflicted pain . . . inflicted with impunity because doctors continue to doubt both the reality of infant pain and its significance.' His work with hypnosis makes a strong case for memory of birth into adult life and infants' ability to perceive and feel, both intra- and extrauterine.

Research shows that babies not only have vivid and sensory impressions of their birth, they also remember these in childhood. Anecdotal evidence tells of children who have described scenes of 'masked people' at birth – doctor and nurses. Babies apparently observe the conditions of the birth room (cold, warm, bright, dark, etc.) and evaluate the attitude and behaviour of birth attendants.

'Virtually all babies complain about bright lights, cold rooms and instruments, the noise, rough contact with their sensitive skin, and nearly every medical routine including slaps, injections, eye drops, hard scales, being held in mid-air and handled by strangers. Babies dislike forceps, sometimes fear incubators, and think the masks worn by nurses and doctors make them look "alien". They strenuously object to the way the umbilical cord is cut, not that it hurts necessarily, but they report anxiety about *how* and *when* this vital connection is severed' (Chamberlain). Too often the messages newborns communicate through body language and sound have been ignored.

Many people, medical staff included, still find it hard to accept that babies experience birth consciously, much less that consciousness is present before birth. However, even in utero, 'the preborn within is alert and eavesdropping. One of the earliest hints of attentive fetal listening can be seen in intrauterine photos of a prenate, eyes sealed but looking profoundly absorbed, delicately holding the umbilical cord. This cord links the solitary womb with the surrounding world . . . Ever-present, it is a handy plaything but alive, changing, and flooded with information. This lively conduit may be a biofeedback unit from which the baby gains information about the flow of nutrients and the slowing or speeding of circulation, a type of maternal–fetal monitor that carries reassuring or worrisome news' (Chamberlain). This 'touch-tone equipment', as Chamberlain calls it, is the agent of connection that links the baby to placenta and mother.

He believes that the foetus is attentive to the 'life-and-death messages passing through the cord' and speculates that 'some kind of intelligence is gained through a combination of touch and hearing.' Touch, a well-developed sense highly visible after birth – the baby touches, tastes, grasps, pokes, and shakes things – acts as a two-way communication: bringing information in – 'How does it taste, feel, sound?' – and sending out – 'I want, I don't want'. Even in utero, touch is present: babies have been observed (with ultrasound) holding the cord or stroking the placenta and burying into it like a pillow (Noble). Chamberlain found in interviews with adults under hypnosis that, coming from an environment of extreme closeness (literally 'touched on all sides'), they would complain of feeling 'lost in space' when born.

Implications of interference in birth

In contrast to the medical model, which relegates the baby to a passive role, babies feel that they are active participants in the birthing process. 'I'm moving', 'I am being supported', 'I did it myself' are positive birth experiences that give a person confidence in their own abilities. If their attempts at being born are thwarted, babies feel powerless. Interference in the birthing process such as the use of forceps, drugs given to the mother, induced birth, Caesarean section, all contribute to the feeling of not having fully participated.

Feelings that emerge in therapy about the birthing process may range from 'I'm stuck' (in the birth canal) to 'I have no support' (drugs administered to the mother) and 'I was forced' (forceps/induced birth). Often comparison with parental memories will later confirm these events. In the baby, the physiological experience finds expression in a corresponding psychological state. Advocating Leboyer's methods of allowing the cord to stop pulsing naturally, Chamberlain observes that babies 'cry more frequently after cords are cut early, less when cords are cut late. Babies react with panic when the umbilical cord becomes compressed or gets wound around the neck. They know when they are losing consciousness and fear the outcome.' Their awareness is attuned to their circumstances – babies are aware what is happening in their own body and even in their environment, and they show their awareness through sound and movement. The first reaction is a coping mechanism. The sense of empowerment or powerlessness, as the case may be, lays down a primary imprint. This imprint lingers in the psyche, becoming a tendency or predisposition that carries over into adult development. People in therapy often find that their behavioural patterns in life correspond with the primary birth imprint.

Cord and placenta symbolism

We can distinguish two main issues that arise from current birth practices: cutting the cord (the act of separation), and discarding the placenta (the loss of sustenance). Although the act of cutting the cord implies the loss of the placenta, they each carry a different symbolic meaning. Cutting the cord is associated with issues of separation and loneliness, whereas discarding the placenta is associated with issues of abandonment and loss of security. Psychologically, the cord represents father issues, whereas the placenta represents mother issues.

In dreams, the placenta is often represented by trees (tree of life), mother's breasts, the earth, an eating vessel, or an androgynous person. The umbilical cord is symbolised by snakes, snakes twisted around legs (arteries), connecting rope, a flagpole, and other connecting devices (Noble).

Placenta issues: control/supply

In German the word for placenta is *Mutterkuchen* ('mother cake'). This term describes the organ's nourishing function for the baby in utero. When the baby is born and begins to exist outside of the mother's body, the placenta's function is considered to be obsolete. However, the newborn experiences being separated from the organ with which it has been connected for nine months as a loss. The moment it emerges from the womb it is deprived not only of the safe haven, but also of the tangible link to the placenta. The loss of blood, which would otherwise flow through the umbilical cord, is a loss of nourishment for the baby. Studies have shown that physiologically, there is an increased risk of anaemia, allergies, asthma, and other chronic afflictions when the cord is cut early. Psychologically, the physiological loss is associated with lack of nourishment, a feeling of 'not getting enough', which may accompany a person throughout life. The sudden loss of control over one's own resources (controlling the bloodflow through the umbilical cord) can effect a lack of confidence in one's own ability to support oneself. All the functions that have empowered the baby in utero are suddenly withdrawn and it is utterly dependent on the mother.

A retained placenta at birth is often associated with the feeling of 'unfinished business', procrastination or being able to do only one thing at a time, take one step at a time. There is a need for completion in an organic way, without outside interference. Time is precious and there is never enough of it. These people often find themselves completing projects under pressure. The risk of a retained placenta is heightened with early cord cutting.

Laing observed that people in therapy have felt physical pain in the placenta even after the placenta and cord were separated, similar to the phantom-pain phenomenon of an amputated limb. He wrote, 'I am impressed by the fact that "I" was once placenta, umbilical cord, and foetus . . . all cellularly, biologically, physically, *genetically, me*'. This unity of feeling, still intact in utero, comes to an abrupt end with birth and separation from cord and placenta.

Noble recommends that parents should consult the newborn about the right time to cut the cord and wait even until after pulsing in the cord has ceased. Referring to the placenta as the 'genetically identical "partner" and long-time intimate companion', she advises parents to give the baby time to release the connection to its 'double'.

Cord issues: bonding/separation

The importance of bonding at birth has been debated ever since its conceptualisation in the sixties. What is the right amount of time for bonding? the experts pondered. Hospital birth has done away with the unlimited time for privacy and intimacy with the newborn that homebirth had afforded parents until the 1940s.

Immediate contact with the mother after delivery is the most important factor in making a newborn feel safe and wanted; whereas separation from the mother after birth is one of the most traumatic events. Cordcutting, as part of the separation trauma, forces the baby to suddenly breathe or else suffocate. In reliving birth in therapy, people have experienced a sharp pain in the navel, loss of breath, fear of death or castration. Noble writes of an 'umbilical crisis' that can arise when the cord is cut postpartum. 'Cutting the cord too soon, together with separating the baby from the mother, is a double injury.'

If the cord is cut too soon, the baby will experience a circulatory and a respiratory shock. A washback effect from blood that would have returned to the mother will put stress on the heart and deprive the baby of oxygen and red blood cells. At the same time the baby needs to take in oxygen in its newly expanded lungs (Noble). Psychologically, fighting for air leads to panic and a sense of insecurity (life is not safe). It may also instill a fight-or-flight reaction (life is a struggle). When the source of oxygen changes abruptly from umbilicus to lungs, this can be associated with fears of smothering later in life or in dreams. 'Fears of cutting and blood phobias may be traced back to the cutting of the cord, as can fear of operations' (Noble). Michel Odent observes that the custom of separating babies from their mothers at birth creates warriors and is perpetuated in warrior-like cultures.

The cord joining the baby to the placenta represents our feeling of connection, of relating to others, or lack thereof. The computer mouse and cord connecting us to 'the world out there' on the Internet, the mobile phone connecting us to other people, are both symbols of our yearning for connection. 'Are you wired for sound?' asks a poster showing a microphone plugged into a representation of earth viewed from space. We want to 'plug in', 'be connected', precisely because fundamentally we lack a sense of connection. When the cord is gone, our first friend, the placenta, is gone. We long to know that we are not alone.

Our Western consumer society is built on an inherent sense of deprivation and trauma and the current birth practices support this dynamic. Our deprivation starts at birth and is continued with feeding patterns. Being fed on demand, the baby 'controls' the breast. This control begins in utero, where the baby is an active partner in regulating the bloodflow from the placenta, not a passive 'consumer'. Being fed on schedule takes away the baby's sense of self-determination. Furthermore, formula feeding instils a predisposition for fast foods: they are always the same (McDonalds); whereas breastmilk tastes different every day, depending on the weather, or what the mother has eaten. Advertising for Coca Cola promises 'the real thing' (breastmilk!). A false sense of security and fulfilment is thus developed.

Integration

Lotus Birth, because of the care taken with the cord and placenta, provides a time for bonding. If the cord is allowed to wither as it is exposed to air, a smooth transition from womb to earth, from water to air, is achieved. Leaving the cord and placenta attached for several days gives mother and baby time to be, to relax. It extends the birth time and allows for integration of the birth experience itself and of the new member into the family.

With gentle birth, water birth and Lotus Birth, whether in birthing centres or at home, babies can be born into this world in a more welcoming way. They can be brought up more psychologically whole. The neuroses that drive many of us would presumably be absent from these children, and from society.

What is presented as developmental psychology today is in fact a description of pathology based on the modern western methods of birth. If birth were made a less traumatic event, much of modern psychology might become obsolete and society might be a collective of healthier, happier individuals.   ❦

Placental psychology

Renuka Potter

W E generally attach little or no importance to our placenta and our relationship to it. The notion that I may have been affected by my relationship with my placenta and the way that relationship ended seemed bizarre when I first encountered it not long ago. And yet, finding images of it in my dreams, reading about it, and revisiting it in meditation and rebirthing/trance sessions, I am now convinced that my placenta is a reality in my psyche. I hope to convey some of the powerful insight I have found through this inner exploration of my relationship with my placenta.

Do pre-birth experiences have an impact?

As a transpersonal psychologist influenced by the work of Stanislav and Christina Grof, Rudolph Steiner and many others, I was already familiar with the psychological impact of the way we were born into this world. I found there an extremely useful adjunct to the mysterious eastern concept of *karma* I had encountered in my studies of meditation. The notions of 'coex systems' (systems of 'condensed experience', Grof) and 'primary imprint' both refer to the phenomenon that a predisposition to respond in particular emotional ways to situations that threaten us in certain ways can often be traced back to a particular feature of our own birth. For example, as a forceps birth I find it difficult to sustain my own inner impetus to finish appropriate tasks. Instead I look for help and encouragement from others, even when I already have all the skills and information I need to complete. And a deadline always helps, with my inclination being to leave it until the last moment (as in writing this!). Furthermore, I had always been puzzled as to why I often went against the help given to me even though I simply *had* to have it. Now I see that my need for help was not because I was *in fact* unable to complete the task, but rather because I had a predisposition to expect that I could not finish a project all by myself. That predisposition seems to be linked with the experience I had in my rebirthing that I was unable to complete my birthing process without outside help. Before the forceps intervention I had lost all hope that the birth would be completed. I felt there was an obstacle I could not get around without help.

The personal experience during a breathwork session of being able to recall my original birth into this body had a profound impact on me because it convinced me that the memory of my birth lives on in my unconscious. For me, this implies also that other memories of which I am normally unconscious live within me. Not only that, but the feelings that accompanied my re-experience of my birth were extremely familiar to me – they were feelings that punctuate my life, making me choose to act in certain ways rather than others at crucial times. These sorts of experiences, involving links between the contents of my unconscious and the patterns of my life, have prepared me for the possibility that my relationship with my placenta and the way in which that relationship was ended may have an effect that plays itself out in my life.

A most intimate relationship

The most important and obvious aspect of placental psychology concerns the closeness and exclusivity of the relationship between the foetus and the placenta. They share the physically limited environment of the womb, always close to each other and close to mother's inner sounds and feelings. The relationship between them is completely symbiotic – one cannot exist without the other. Not only that, but they come from completely identical genetic material – from the fertilisation of the same egg and sperm. That is, their cellular structure is the same, the same DNA. They share an identical resonance.

The drawings of uterine consciousness collected by Grof suggest that we have some level of consciousness even while we are still in our mother's body. In deep trance it is quite possible to connect with the oceanic feelings of that early stage of our development into full human consciousness. Mott makes a case for the basis of this consciousness being the flow of fluids between the foetus and placenta, and Chamberlain interprets evidence of the foetus holding its cord as suggesting that the foetus can regulate the flow to some extent (or at least be aware of it). Be that as it may, there is no reason to assume that any consciousness that exists belongs only to the baby. It is likely that foetus and placenta have a *shared* consciousness while fluids are being transferred between them. After birth, of course, it is only the baby that can survive and grow into full human consciousness. The placenta, having completed its task of support, withdraws from life into death.

If the death of the placenta is allowed to happen naturally, as this book advocates, it is likely that there is a flow of more than blood from the placenta to the baby after birth – there is also likely to be a transfer of consciousness. I would like to suggest that the placenta after birth holds the most deeply earthy and unconscious part of the joint psyche – the part that is least linked to consciousness of individuality, a form of collective unconscious that is particularly related to ancestry.

Why Lotus Birth is so important

Birth is much more difficult for the baby than for its placenta because of its size, its bony skeleton and so forth. It is quite likely that the trauma of birth causes the baby to lose its hold on the deep consciousness of itself as a being grounded in placental/ earth consciousness, the unconscious wisdom of the body, the mammalian brain, as Odent puts it in the foreword to this book. If the cord is not cut, this familiar wisdom or sense of being that still resonates in the placenta can be accessed by the baby. Birth does not disturb the consciousness of the placenta because the placenta does not have to struggle to take a breath as does the baby, nor does it have sense receptors that are bombarded by strange unfamiliar sensations. Being still connected to the placenta after birth allows the baby to reconnect with its former sense of inner stability, of connection to a deep unchanging reality. It can remember the familiar resonance of deep unconscious knowing that still resides in the placenta.

For this connection to occur we need to allow babies time after birth. When a baby is not given time he or she cannot relate deeply with the knowing residing in the placenta. Not allowing time is a contemporary disease – we cannot stop hurrying. Lack of time to strengthen ourselves after birth from the energy of the placenta may be a primary imprint for the feeling that we do not have enough time in life. Allowing time after birthing also allows for the sacredness of birth to be recognised. We more clearly see the miracle that birth is when we have time to gaze, to hold, to touch.

Mott also talks about the incorporation of the placenta into the psyche of the baby. He describes a process that begins with the first breath, when the placenta is felt as the lungs that allow the nourishing first breath, the throat is felt as the cord and the brain or head is now the baby/foetus. This model is fascinating in that it is based on his findings in the deep intra-psychic work with his patients and himself. That is, it is what he *found*. However, two things are notable, one that it takes the early cutting of the cord (the male medical model) for granted, and the other that the placenta is *felt* by the psyche to be internalised after birth.

In the case of a Lotus Birth there is less pressure on the baby to breathe immediately, and the transition between the intrauterine environment and condition of utter dependence to the first steps of independence outside the womb is not as severe and threatening. The placenta is psychologically akin to the mother who is there for the toddler exploring the environment – the toddler ventures forth happily in a new environment as long as the mother is there for frequent returns to the reassurance of her presence. To some extent, it is simply the *presence* of the placenta that is important, as Rachana discovered with newborns whose cords were cut when their placenta was physically moved away from them.

When the placenta remains connected to the baby after birth, the baby internalises a sense of deep connection to its physical being and the knowing that is in the mammalian and reptilian brains (see Pearce). With a Lotus Birth, the baby can draw into itself the deep sense of connection to the fact of embodiment, its composition of blood, bones, muscles and other tissue – it can experience its complete incorporation. This then becomes the knowing on which its sense of being is based. This deep knowing lends it a security, a reassurance of being what it is. When our connection with the fact of our physical being is firm, we are then free to become aware of what lies beyond – the higher levels of existence. We become better able to experience ourselves as bodies of light and energy beyond the dense reality of the physical body (Daricha). We are open to inspiration, to higher guidance, to insight.

What the placenta stands for

From my reading, my own dreams, imagination and deep meditational trance experiences it seems to me that the placenta has various additional meanings. Firstly, my placenta stands for the recognition of my true nature by another. The placenta knows me better than anyone else ever has or ever will. Perhaps even better than I know myself. This is because my placenta knew me from the very start of my existence as this individual. Not only that, but at the beginning of my existence, my placenta was bigger and therefore more mature than I was.

Secondly, because my placenta knows me better than I know myself, and because my placenta feeds me and deals with my waste, my placenta symbolises my inner wisdom. This inner wisdom is my link to the wisdom of my ancestry too, due to the fact that it carries my identical DNA in an undiluted, unable-to-be-contaminated form (because it has no independent consciousness). In this sense, my placental knowledge is similar to animal or mammalian knowledge, and it is my experience that it can be used as a bridge to my own unconscious knowing in a similar way to an animal totem.

Thirdly, and perhaps most obviously, my placenta embodies my first relationship. All those months in utero when we alone inhabited that watery space we communicated through touch, through sharing food and waste, through circulating blood and energy. We were joined intimately through this shared life-blood, and yet there was a definite separation between my placenta and I that was mediated and measured through the cord. I could move independently whereas my placenta could not, and yet I was completely dependent on my placenta and forced to share everything except the new cells being continually grown within my body. In turn, it shared with me the nutrients it received from our mother, except for those prevented by the placental barrier. It has been called the 'dark twin' and my survival in the womb was completely dependent upon it. It is my 'other half' in the most absolute of symbiotic relational terms, because without it I was completely unable to survive.

The effects of cutting the cord

If the above are some of the characteristics of the relationship between a person and their placenta, what is the effect of cutting the cord soon after the baby is born? If my placenta is that which knows me best, then its loss will entail losing my sense of being knowable and recognisable for who I really am. I will feel as though I am among strangers who can never know me, and it is possible I may feel that I was born into a family of people who are alien to me – a not uncommon feeling for children.

I will be divorced from my deep inner knowing. One of the ways this may manifest, especially if accompanied by additional birth trauma, could be through a person failing to inhabit their body completely. Such a person may daydream excessively, may try to please others rather than operating from their own inner impetus. It may lead to a feeling of being lost and always having to search for answers to life's riddles, leading to a deep restlessness in the soul.

Loss of relationship with our placenta may set the scene for a whole series of relationship losses throughout our lives. We may find ourselves cutting off from the best and most intimate relation-ships. We may not be conscious of why, but we may be aware of a fear that we may be abandoned. The loss of the relationship with the placenta may be played out in our relationship with our mother, with our siblings, with our best friends, with our lovers. Eventually, if we are lucky, we realise we are being driven by an unconscious need that is actually ruining our chances for true relationship. Awareness being the key to change, the situation then has a chance of resolving itself.

Reconnecting

What difference does a Lotus Birth make? As Mott points out, after birth the ideal situation would be that a baby gradually withdraws its own recognition, knowledge and relationship from the placenta into itself. This would happen first on a physical level with the nourishment left in the placenta flowing naturally into the baby. Then it would happen in terms of feelings, with the feeling of safety and trust that surrounds being recognised for who I truly am. If I know myself on this level, I can rely on the feelings I get from my body to guide my behaviour in the world. I am not vulnerable.

A dream I had while preparing for writing this illustrates the meaning of the placenta for me.

I watch people in a river being carried quickly along. It goes over a waterfall and takes the people with it.

Now there's something I need to buy. I go to the shop and at the entrance I see a woman with whom I had a close relationship that was ended abruptly and unsatisfactorily. We look into each other's eyes as I pass her and I know she knows me better than anyone else does. The shop is round and filled with all sorts of things in a higgledy-piggledy array. What I need is on a higher floor but I cannot resist looking at all the things available.

The river is the birth process with its powerful inescapable energy. The shop is the placenta where everything a baby needs is available. The woman at the entrance who knows me so well represents the intimate relationship I had with my placenta – a relationship that can never be repeated and yet one I yearn for. It feels good that there is that deep recognition from her – it still exists somewhere.

All our lives we are searching to find again the perfection represented by our relationship with our placenta. Searching for the placenta is like searching for God. In fact, the placenta is God. Now that is absurd. However, when a person is given a Lotus Birth, the value of the placenta and what it represents – the perfect relationship, true recognition and mirroring – are internalised. That is, God is internalised. This insight that what we are looking for is within us exists in all religions. For those who have the cord cut early, though, the search for God takes precedence over all other endeavours. When we know that God is within us we can rest in a deep sense that all is okay.

When the cord is not cut

The sense of loss that is initiated by loss of the placenta cannot be soothed by outer relationships. There is something within us that will not be satisfied no matter how good a relationship appears to be – compared to that original relationship it lacks depth of knowing, intimacy and communication. It can only be healed by a person returning to a deep sense of self-sufficiency through meditation, depth psychology and the like. Or by allowing time for the connection between baby and placenta at birth to terminate naturally, by mutual agreement, when the relationship has been completed – as in a Lotus Birth.

The simple process of leaving the placenta attached to the baby until it drops off, signalling a completion of the transfer of matter and consciousness, reveals itself as one of the most profound and revolutionary possibilities of human life. Seeing babies who were born with Lotus Birth has left me with the conviction that these babies are whole – they have something that in most of us is only potential. Somehow an aspect of their being seems to be at the end of a road I personally am just completing – the journey to complete embodiment. It is only through complete embodiment that we human beings can heal ourselves and the earth. We need to master this to allow human life on earth to continue. These lotus babies, in my opinion, hold the key to our future survival, for they are deeply connected to earth wisdom and can allow the light of consciousness to be brought through to this dense physical level.

Placenta - our connection with the earth

A fit end to the process of Lotus Birth, from the point of view of the psyche, would entail returning the placenta to the earth with which it resonates most profoundly. The burying of the placenta in the earth is a ritual of many cultures. In Australia we are fortunate to have as a model the Australian Aborigines whose birthing practices, until recent medical intervention, have allowed them to be aware of themselves as completely embodied in their earth nature. Their whole psychology, as expressed in and through the Dreamtime, asserts their oneness with the earthy expressions of nature – even landforms are embodied in the same way as themselves. Where an individual's placenta is buried marks their particular link to the earth and its dreaming. Living in Aboriginal Central Australia in the early seventies allowed me to glimpse this truth, and my connection with Daricha and Rachana in the late nineties has allowed me to understand the extra dimension I saw in their existence thirty years ago.

It is my conviction that taking time to birth our children naturally with awareness of them as sentient beings at a vulnerable stage in their embodiment will encourage greater manifestation of human potential. People with Lotus Births will find it easier to have supportive loving relationships that end naturally rather than when neurotic needs or fears are triggered. Lotus birthing will also go a long way toward healing the split between humans and the earth that has become a feature of 'advanced' human cultures. When we can feel and know our energetic link to the earth we will be unable to exploit and destroy it.

At first glance, it seems unlikely that the relationship we had with our placenta and the way that relationship was ended, could have such far-reaching effects. However, if we can be open to the possibility and examine our own psychic contents through dreams and trance-inducing therapies, we will find that we are indeed creatures of the earth, connected through the intrauterine relationship with our placenta. The psyche has taken a detour through the possibility that mind is supreme and body is a hindrance. It is now time to reclaim our link with our bodies, as physical embodiment allows us to reach greater heights and achieve greater potential than is possible through our disembodied minds.

Chapter 6

Matters of life and birth

Dr Christopher Millar

Dr Christopher Millar, MD, explored the experience of having his umbilical cord cut in primal therapy. Primal therapy is a way of entering the world of the unconscious via the emotions. It has been found that emotions experienced in daily life are rooted in past events. Where there has been a lack of expression, the emotion continues to live on in the unconscious, which in turn resides in the body and then becomes an ongoing influence on future events with similar components. The location of and expression of these emotions can have a dramatic effect on people's lives and bring insights to behaviour patterns and dispel old belief systems.

Birth is a crucial event for us and is an ongoing influence in how we live our lives. In the following excerpt from his book Dr Millar describes reliving the cutting of his umbilical cord and the life patterns that developed from that event.

My placenta - Disposable friend

HAVE you ever thought about your placenta? I've thought about mine – every time I delivered a baby and had to measure, weigh, and describe the placenta. I would think: for nine months of my life I had a placenta, which was 'cellularly,

biologically, physically, *genetically, me*' (RD Laing). What did that
part of me mean to me? And how does its loss affect me?

Every time I disposed of a placenta from the baby I had just
delivered into the machine that minced it up into unrecognisable
pieces, I felt what a pity such a wonderful friend and companion
had come to this end.

Why do we measure the length, width, depth of the placenta?
Weigh it, describe it, count the number of vessels in the cord, measure the cord length? And write it all down as if it meant something?

It is not science: it is a ritual. Just like a funeral is a ritual. We
all had a placenta once upon a time: it was our life source, at the
end of our cord. Every day we touched it, and we knew we were
touching ourselves. It pulsed, it was alive.

Does anyone doubt that we carry some memory of that part
of ourselves?

Does anyone doubt that every time we measure, weigh, and
describe a baby's placenta we are symbolically also saying good-bye
to our own?

Because in all probability we never had the opportunity to
deal with our placenta for ourselves, to say good-bye, at the time of
own birth.

RD Laing asks: 'Could we be haunted by our placenta: our
intrauterine twin, lover, rival, double? Could the placenta be the
original life-giver, life-sucker: our first friend or our first persecutor/
tormentor?'

I did a drawing of my cat and myself: I drew the cat almost as
a reflection of myself, a sort of mirror-image, as if it had a reciprocal
anatomical relationship with me. Might not our relationships with
our pets somehow reflect our relationship with our placenta: that
this relationship with our pet allows us first to ease the pain of that
loss, then on the death of the pet to come to terms with the actual
loss, to resolve the grief we feel from the loss of our placenta?

Placental cat   Painting: Dr Christopher Millar

Another drawing I did to depict womb-life more consciously depicted the foetus–cord–placenta growing like a tree on a mountain. The analogy was so obvious in the drawing that it did not occur to me that it was symbolic in any way.

As Laing has noted:

soil	–	womb	–	context
roots	–	placenta	–	other
trunk	–	cord	–	connection
tree	–	foetus	–	self

The ancient Egyptians use the symbol of the placenta in their hieroglyphic alphabet (Gardiner). It represents the sound 'ch', as in the Scottish word 'loch'.

In the English language there are three words whose connection with each other is indicated by the combination of the letters 'gr': green, grass, grow. The 'gr' sound somehow signifies green grassy growth, and equates them one with another.

Laing mentions that he has been told that 'thought' is represented in Egyptian hieroglyphics by the image of the heart.

In a language where the written word is so obviously derived from the symbolic thought processes of the infant (Latin: *infans*, speechless), might not words containing the 'ch' sound, represented by a pictographic symbol of the placenta, somehow reflect feelings, thoughts, attitudes, about the placenta? I think so.

Here is a list of words that I feel are 'placental' in some way:

give pleasure to

friend

to travel downstream

plan, counsel, will, way of acting

night

require, demand

suffer, bear patiently

wide, broad

tower, fortress

join together, unite

be beneficial/advantageous

sunshine

horizon

reap

he who goes after,
accompanies

river bank

things, property

dusk, twilight	
to live; life	
nourish	
quench	
depart, loosen	
fasten	
clothing	
resting-place	
defend, protect	
learn, become acquainted with, know	
rob, despoil	
manager	
with, near	

in front of, face to face

How did the list of words affect you? Do you agree that they are 'placental' in nature? If not, what words to you think/feel are placental in some way?

What does your placenta mean to you?

Separation after birth – Death and her friends

Our first separation, for most of us, is from our placenta, which is, as I have already pointed out, genetically identical to ourselves.

The process and drama of birth overshadows the delivery and disposal of the placenta: any proper farewell is impossible. Almost before we catch our first breath the umbilical cord is cut and tied and our placenta is removed from us, measured and disposed of. At the time we are pre-occupied with our newly-required breathing apparatus. The placenta has been superseded by the lungs, and there is no time to reconcile ourselves to its redundancy.

As a foetus in utero we know our placenta by two features: its structure, which is its physical presence; and its function, which is its response to foetal demands of oxygen, nutrients and waste elimination. When that function ceases, and when that structure is no longer accessible, we cannot immediately conceive of its existence. We need time to come to our own conclusion that we can relinquish this structure, this part of ourselves, because it no longer has a useful function. It is a sad, yet honest, decision to give up our one and only possession.

The honesty and generosity involved with this partial self-sacrifice cannot be exhibited if the placenta has been taken away before we realise that its function has ceased.

There are therefore two crucial steps in separating from our placenta. The first step must allow enough time for the placenta to stop functioning and the baby to initiate her (or his) own respiration. That means that the placenta be still attached when the baby takes her (or his) first breath. Whether the baby breathes before the placenta stops pulsating, or vice versa, is for the baby and the placenta to decide. The next crucial step is the act of separation, which does not mean the act of cutting and tying the cord so much as the removal of the placenta from the vicinity of the baby so that actual contact is no longer possible. When that is best timed is a matter of intuitive judgement: when you feel it is time.

What happens when such separation takes place before time? Consider the difference between having five years to decide for yourself that a painful deformed arthritic finger needs removal; and

---

How did I leave thee?
Let me count the vessels

The ship of my mind
Gave berth to an ideal
I would love the life I'd left in time
In time
Regretting nothing feeling everything

Out of port I turned to rum
And drank myself
Silly
Forgetting everything feeling nothing

I promised myself to reform
Yes I would reform
No man can land who hasn't sailed
Nor sell himself for money or love

We're in this together my friend I said
And my foothold on life hangs by a thread

---

being told in a casualty department that the finger you have just crushed in an accident will have to be removed in an emergency operation. Consider analogous situations for an arm or leg; part of your brain; a loved one.

Imagine what it is like for a baby to be allowed no say in the amputation of a body part which was for so long perceived to be integral part of life. Consider that this right to self-determination is denied at a most harrowing and stressful time in life: the first thing that happens after having endured the death of birth is that they take away the only foot-hold on life, your best friend. Not even a chance to say good-bye.

As long as you
Are mine and I am your reason for existing
Then life is a piece of cake

The conversation was non-existent
Our exchange was richer than that
Give and take like barter and trade
And the feeling of love in between

Life has been more pleasant
But I don't remember when
Certainly not since
Will it ever again

I can't remember when we said good-bye
I'm not even sure that we did
But I know in my heart there was love in his blood
And I feel in my bones that he lives and grows
In my mind

Dr Christopher Millar

The baby will miss the placenta for the rest of her (or his) life, in the same way that the loved ones of people missing and presumed dead, and whose bodies are never found, never quite accept that loss. Without evidence of death, proof of structure without function, it doesn't seem real. It is too late after the event to explain to a baby what has happened: she (or he) must do things in her (or his) own time, as it happens, and in her (or his) own way.

Separation from our placenta, as it is commonly practised in our society today, is the single biggest threat to the maintenance of contact with our genetic reality. Not only because our placenta is genetically identical with us, but because the manner of that separation is such an unexpected and heartless exercise. The only way for a baby to cope with such brutality is to deny it ever happened. The event never happened, my placenta never existed, I deny the existence of that part of me. Who can say how much that denial limits our potential to grow and to communicate with our self and others? Who cares?

Cutting my cord - Subscriber trunk dialing ignored

Scene 1: I ring up my girlfriend, wanting to see her: we are in the process of separating after a long, close relationship. She won't see me: she is going somewhere. She hangs up, and I am left with the phone gone dead in my hand. I am upset. I feel alienated.

I recount the event in therapy, express the feeling: 'Please let me see you again, don't cut me out of your life, don't cut me off. I need you.'

Horrible diffuse peri-umbilical ache. Feeling of need, loneliness, isolation, despair, alienation. I still needed that communication with my mother via my cord and placenta when they cut it off. So senseless and so heartless. Who were they?

Scene 2: Two days later, in group therapy: someone next to me in pain comes to lie on my tummy. I am thinking about my placenta: I wonder where it went to?

'I could lie here all day using your tummy as a pillow,' says the someone.

'No you couldn't,' I think to myself, threatened by the closeness of physical contact, resentful of his presumption and familiarity. I wish he would just piss off, but I do not say so. I diffuse my discomfort by joking:

'You'll get an umbilical cord stump in your ear if you do.'

The someone senses my inability to respond to his affection, and replies:

'Right on!'

This expression annoys me, always has. I think: 'Right on? Why not: Left on?' I am sensitive to such expressions, being of a sinister bent, sometimes even gauche or maladroit.

It hits me like a hammer: LEFT ON!

All week I have been leaving things 'left on': the jug boiled over, I burnt the toast, I let the soup burn on the stove. All my life I have periodically done the same.

Always things that plug in, provide food or warmth.

As a foetus in the womb I was always connected: by the placental plug into the uterine socket. I didn't have to worry about switching anything off: it was all done for me. I was warm, and fed.

I didn't have to learn to switch anything off till after I was born; but I was deprived of that learning experience. I was deprived of the opportunity of taking responsibility for myself: they switched me off, they cut my cord, took away my initiative.

Who the hell were they!

Scene 3: A certain maternity hospital, the faceless administration thereof, do not like me parking my bike in their grounds. They leave me a note (unsigned and type-written) threatening to cut off my lock and chain and impound by bike.

My bike is special to me: it sits between my legs like my penis (which they circumcised), like my cord (which they cut).

I am angry: They have no RIGHT! I want it LEFT ON!

See the parallel?

Who are you anyway?

Chapter 7

The benefits of Lotus Birth

The term 'Lotus Birth' was coined by Clair Lotus Day who, when pregnant and living in California, questioned many doctors about the need to cut the cord. Finding an obstetrician sympathetic to her quest, she gave birth to her son Trimurti in San Francisco in 1974 and took him home soon after with his cord uncut.

Since then, many babies in many countries have been born in this way, including babies born at home, in hospital and even by Caesarean section.

Dr Sarah Buckley, *Pregnancy* magazine, Spring 1998

The amazing placenta: The tree of life

Pacia Sallomi

WHAT have you heard about the placenta? Have you heard that it looks like a piece of liver? Have you heard about the 'tree of life' formed by the foetal vessels? Have you heard the placenta described as the sustainer of life for your growing baby?

Our culture tends to look at the placenta either with scientific awe, or with no respect at all. It has been thought of merely as an anchor for the cord and as a sieve of passive transport to the 'parasitic' foetus. We now know these ideas to be false. The placenta is the organ of life – sustaining and nurturing the growing foetus until it is ready for independent existence. It is *active* and *selective* in its transfer of substances. It is a 'biological microcosm' able to perform functions of the alimentary, pulmonary, renal, hepatic and endocrine systems both *for* and *in collaboration with* the foetus. The placenta also affects and regulates many of the maternal body functions through its syntheses of hormones. And finally, all of this must be accomplished while maintaining an equilibrium between the foetus and the mother.

The placenta and foetus both arise from the same cell, the fertilised ovum. After ovulation, progesterone production is increased. This acts to facilitate cell division, as the fertilised egg travels down the fallopian tube and prepares the uterine lining for its nourishment. By the sixth or seventh day after fertilisation the egg begins to implant in the uterus. This implantation is facilitated by the production of oestrogen and prostaglandins by the mother, and is maintained by hormones produced in the *corpus luteum* (ovary) and later by the placenta.

The egg (called the trophoblast at this stage) becomes completely embedded in the endometrium (uterine lining). Maternal blood pools are created around the implantation site to give nourishment to the growing embryo. At this point a rudimentary 'cord stump' is already present. Specified cells of the embryo then form projections (called villi) that burrow into these maternal blood pools, which begin formation of the foetal circulation within what will become the placenta.

The 'invasion' of the egg into the endometrium elicits changes within the uterine lining. Maternal blood supply is greatly increased

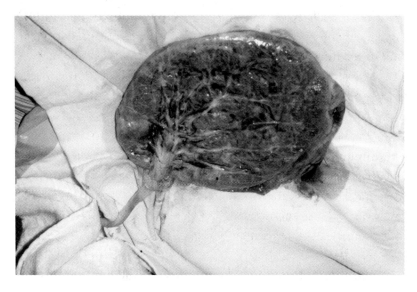

The 'tree of life'   Photo: Dr Sarah Buckley

and enters the placenta, passing next to a membrane separating foetal and maternal circulation, where exchange of substances (nutrients, wastes, etc) occurs. Thus while foetal and maternal circulation remain separate, the bond has already been formed between mother and child. At birth the cord still pulsates its connection, and in the minutes that follow this intimate exchange becomes transferred from placental site to eyes and arms and breasts.

Throughout history there have been varying beliefs and attitudes regarding the placenta, its significance and its disposal. Generally it has been the traditional midwife who has acted as guardian of rituals surrounding the birth process. As societies have become more technical in their viewpoints toward life, however, these rites and rituals tend to be discarded.

In some countries the midwife is an influential and powerful woman of the community, while in others she and her work are considered dirty and of the lower caste. The position of the midwife may be some indication of the relative value placed upon childbirth in that culture, and is related to its attitudes toward the placenta, toward menses, and toward womanhood. In India, Pakistan and Bangladesh, menstrual blood, the placenta, and blood of childbirth are considered ritually polluting and symbolically dangerous substances. Midwifery is one of the 'unclean', lower caste tasks, along with burying the dead, working with products of dead animals such as leather, cleaning the streets and emptying bucket latrines. It is common in the Middle East for a midwife to give a ritual cleansing bath to the woman five to ten days after delivery. Even though her social status is low, she is recognised and respected for her ritualistic importance in the life of women.

Disposal of the placenta also takes on ritualistic significance and is often the duty of the midwife. In some developing countries this practice maintains the status of the midwife in the community because the modern maternity units commonly reject traditional birth rituals. In Malaysia, the child and placenta are considered to be siblings. Since it is thought that the two are reunited at death, the *kampong bidan* (midwife) carefully washes the placenta, cord and membrane and wraps them in a white cloth to be buried.

In our culture the placenta is often thrown out with the hospital's sterile trash. However, scientists have taken an interest in the utilisation of the placenta for experimentation, and it has been found that the membranes are valuable in the healing of burn patients. It is used in some cosmetics; have you tried placenta shampoo? A fairly common ritual is to bury the placenta under a tree or in the garden.

The Lotus placenta

Alice Scholes

IN utero the placenta is an amazing 'biological microcosm'. It is able to perform functions of the alimentary, pulmonary, renal, hepatic and endocrine systems, both for and in collaboration with the foetus. It also affects and regulates many of the maternal body functions through its synthesis of hormones.

The placenta and foetus both arise from the same cell – the fertilised ovum. Here is how that happens: after ovulation, progesterone production is increased. This acts to facilitate cell division as the fertilised egg travels down the fallopian tube and prepares the uterine lining for nourishment. By the sixth or seventh day after fertilisation, the egg begins to implant in the uterus. This implantation is facilitated by the production of oestrogen and prostaglandins by the mother, and is maintained by hormones produced in the ovary and later by the placenta.

The egg becomes completely embedded in the uterine lining. Maternal blood pools are created around the implantation site to give nourishment to the growing embryo. At this point a rudimentary cord stump is already present. Specified cells of the embryo then form projections (villa) which burrow into these maternal blood pools which begin formation of the foetal circulation within what will become the placenta.

The magical placenta is a timed organ. This means it has a specific life span after which it no longer functions. In nature, this life span is completed fully when the cord, attached to placenta and baby, drops away from the baby unassisted. It seems that in utero the placenta has a physical function but once out of the womb, while still attached, its function is purely metaphysical. The cord grows long enough for the baby to be born first with the placenta being sheared off the uterine wall by the contracting action of the uterine muscles which squeeze the baby out. A mother gives birth to a baby and then to a placenta, then placenta and cord leave the baby.

After attending three births in a row several years ago, where two mothers opted to leave the placenta on, I became conscious, for the first time, of cord-cutting as a violent act.

As described, the foetus and placenta arise from the same cell so baby and placenta are one, therefore they share the same etheric field aura. While the placenta remains attached after birth the etheric field around the baby is sealing off properly and when complete, the cord drops away. The complete field results in a stronger immune system because it is stronger field energy.

All the life force of that amazing organ gets transferred along the cord to the baby during this period. To cut the cord is to deprive the baby of a completeness of these powerful subtle forces.

In practical terms leaving the placenta to come away has many unseen advantages. The whole process tends to slow the family down and make it far more conscious of the fact that the baby's spirit is still adjusting to its new home. Family members' etheric aura can be healed by being in contact with the Lotus baby.

More often than not we are thinking of our own discomfort when we don't wish to allow this natural completion to take place. On a deeper level, this discomfort could well be that the process is an acknowledgment that death and birth go hand in hand. The placenta literally dies. For the baby it is the death of what used to be – life in the womb.

It seems to me that the advantages far outweigh the disadvantages when one looks at the short time span involved. I wish to warn the parents who choose to give their baby a Lotus Birth that the reality will likely bring up resistances they were not aware of, in themselves and others, which often results in wanting to cut the cord. If they can try to work through these resistances rather than succumb to them they will have broken through some strong negative conditioning.

Sometimes only one parent wants the placenta left and this often brings a lot of pressure from the other parent. There needs to be a firm agreement before the birth so that the baby does not become the centre of such conflict during these precious days.

When choosing a Lotus Birth it is best to decide on no visitors until the placenta has detached. This period belongs to the family with whom the baby lives, and keeping it free from distractions helps the mother, in particular, to consciously attune to the baby's spirit.

How to care for the intact placenta

It is important to keep the placenta level with the baby after birth until the gelatinous substance (Whorton's jelly) has solidified, hence no more blood transfusion is occurring. After that time, wash the placenta thoroughly, taking care to remove any blood clots as these will begin putrefaction more quickly. The more dry you can keep the placenta, the better, as this will encourage the drying of the cord. Within a few days the cord will naturally fall off at the navel, leaving a gorgeous belly button! There may be a natural break in the cord above the navel, between the navel and the placenta, but as in a cut cord, this stump will eventually break forth on its own.

Jeannine Parvati Baker, *Lotus Birth Information Packet*, available through Freestone Publishing

---

Keeping the unity of pregnancy

Clair Lotus Day

Clair Lotus Day, who described herself as 'a clairvoyant, nurse and teacher', was one of the first who believed that the umbilical cord should not be cut at birth but allowed to fall off naturally with the placenta at around the seventh day after birth, the time when the umbilical stump of a cord that has been cut will usually shrivel and fall away. Clair called this way of birth 'Lotus Birth' and developed elaborate written material describing the spiritual benefits of this method and the psychological harm which may result from cutting the cord. She is regarded by many as the 'Mother of Lotus Birth'.

I HAVE been clairvoyant now for about ten years, and after the birth of my second child my clairvoyance led me more into sightings dealing with health. On more than a hundred occasions I have seen the astral vibration of the umbilical cord being severed and on many different times this vibration occurred when the person was in what one might call a negative state . . . All of these hundred and more instances led me to the belief that possibly the umbilical cord did not necessarily have to be severed. I began thinking more and more about the possibility. I also contacted twenty doctors in obstetrics departments in San Francisco and the government, with replies that severing was done because of custom and cleanliness.

We can change the custom and be clean. I talked with a doctor at the maternity section of Public Health in Berkeley who referred me to the book *In the Shadow of Man* by Jane Goodall, who states that the chimps seem to keep the placenta intact until it comes off naturally. At the back of the book she raises the question 'Why are they as adults so family-oriented?' I, of course, think it is because the cord was not severed at birth, keeping the unity of the pregnancy; mother and child.

I then became pregnant for the sole purpose of having a child in this way.

The doctor with whom I worked for eight and half months, at the last moment before and during my labour (near transition) wanted to take me to the hospital and cut the cord. I released him and was guided. I went to Drs . . . and explained my clairvoyance, that I also had two years of nursing with five years' experience, that I had a small pyramid at home in which to cure the placenta while the cord came off naturally. Dr . . . said that he would consult with the other doctors, but to get myself to the hospital in San Francisco or I would have the baby at the door step, so with hope in my heart and a new being on the way I arrived at the hospital. It was a completely natural birth, the placenta was expelled five minutes after birth. Dr . . . came up to me and said, you look like the kind who would like to go home with the placenta still intact. Praise God. That was the best gift that could ever have been given to me. The

---

Placenta prints

To make a placenta print, first lay the placenta, maternal side down, on a sheet of newspaper. Then make sure there is enough blood on the foetal side to make a print. Arrange the umbilical cord artistically, then press a clean sheet of art paper gently over the placenta and cord. It will dry to a brown colour.

Nan Kochler in: *Midwifery Today* No. 9, 1989

only red tape I had to go through was to sign a piece of paper stating why I did not have the blood test done from the cut cord. I said, for health and religious reasons.

An hour after Trimurti was born I was on my way home, put the placenta in the upper chamber of the pyramid, wrapped his cord with sterile gauze, leaving it straight and horizontal . . . I sat with my heavenly child as his heart system was paved in harmony with what sustained him, which I figuratively and symbolically liken to the tree in the middle (the umbilical cord). He is a most harmonious, strong, healthy, happy, alert child who is bringing completeness and fullness into my life.

A centre opened up in me near the cervix and root chakra, much like a circle – open and full, extending my energy and giving me a total perspective and naturalness. This centrifugal force has kept my energy full and my karma my own.

Lotus Birth fully bloomed

Jeannine Parvati Baker, MA

I T is with much humble joy that we report the full blooming Lotus Birth of my fourth baby, our first son, two years ago (1980). We saw so much value in allowing the cord to break forth on its own! His navel is exceptionally beautiful and his power as a being remains intact. Needless to say, we did not circumcise, or violate in any metallic way his being.

When the third day postpartum arrived, the cord was quite crisp and the temptation to help its brittleness along was strong. We mother-roasted, that is, had a lying-in ceremony of warming up the birth room, like a sauna, and letting both the mama and baby be naked together in warm comfort. However, we didn't break the cord but allowed it to fall away organically. This waiting set the way for subsequent patience in letting old withered parts of the psyche drop off when its inner and organic cycle was complete – a much softer way than the heroic warrior with a sword who cuts away, breaks through defenses and otherwise valiantly wounds the soul. We would allow our son's attachments to let go when their own time was ripe, and the Lotus Birth was the initial testimony to that promise.

Lotus Birth is the maintenance of connection with the afterbirth. Instead of severing the umbilical cord, it is allowed to wither and fall off by itself, usually in two-and-a-half to seven days. The placenta is left connected to the baby and allowed a natural death. Generally once it is washed and dried, it is placed in a bowl bedside. Short cords can pose mobility limitations, and obviously the mother and baby aren't likely to go anywhere until the cord falls off at the navel. Clair Day, founder and researcher of Lotus Birth, refers to this as 'the breaking forth time' and it is a beautiful way to describe that incredibly impressionable, immediate postpartum period.

As a midwife and mother myself, I was attracted to any ritual which might slow down all of us healthy and active women and increase the bonding for the entire family. Clair was quick to testify that the Lotus Birth did indeed appear in other animals. The chimpanzees, who maintain life-long family units and monogamous matings as well as clans, are an example. They do not bite through the umbilicus but carry newborn and placenta until it withers away.

I have chosen to follow this ritual birth process because of a primary understanding of the incredibly vital link which exists between mother and baby. Lotus Birth is a demonstration that all attachments, to placenta, to mother, to earth, will eventually cease of their own accord. My husband said that letting our baby drop off his cord at his own rate helped him to trust the organic rhythms of his son. In midwifery practice I leave it to the parents to cut the umbilical cord, should they desire to do so.

Our son, Gannon Hamilton Baker, arrived at 4.00 a.m. like a cannonball, received into the waiting hands of his chosen parents with his twin sisters alongside. My daughter promptly reminded me to deliver the placenta of her new brother and fetched the bowl for me. Gannon, being my biggest baby yet, had a very large placenta as well and it filled the Blessing Way bowl that I had used in ceremonies for my many pregnant friends. It was the deep green ceramic bowl my mom used to make cookies when I was growing up, and the bowl she gave me when I first established my dwelling apart from her home. The placenta filled it almost to the brim.

After a few hours we rinsed and washed away any residual blood from the placenta and patted it dry as carefully as I might towel off my dear grandmother. In fact, it was my daughter who noted the metaphorical resemblance and began to call the placenta 'Grandmother', in gesture of utmost respect. We were used to calling the moon by this name, so it was a logic extension to call this marvellously vibrant organ, Gannon's first mother, 'Grandmother'.

Babies don't seem to kick or play with the drying cord very much. I remember holding Gannon on my belly most of the time postpartum. Once the cord became stiffer, it was more challenging to move around, although still peaceful, even comfortable.

This 'breaking forth' time is a most precious pause in the fast lane of life. Visitors can be kept to a minium and obviously only the most tolerant and open-minded of friends will be the invited guests. The bonding with mama is fortified during visiting – not many guests will ask to hold your new baby when he is hooked up to 'that thing in the bowl'.

When Gannon's cord fell off three days after birth, we shared an amazing experience. In the early afternoon, as the scent of placenta wafted richly around our redwood forest cabin, I noticed that the cord right at the umbilical end looked very different than it had the last three days. It looked complete. I could see the cord was brittle and was soon to break forth. It did so effortlessly. Our son's cord came away from his belly-button with his family watching, the same loving sisters and papa who were at his birth. At that moment he deliberately reached for his cord, now broken away. It was the first time we had observed him even touching the cord, much less purposefully (as it seemed to us) grab for it and hold it tight. Not even in random movement had he touched his cord before that time. He grasped his departed cord and was perceptibly still. After a long while, he let it go. So simple a release. Each one of us experienced an incredible energy rush. The room filled with light and the sound rang through my ears and our hearts flew open even more (could it be more?) to our first son. It felt like his second birthing. Our baby had now delivered himself. What we saw was the perfect balance of nature – as the new one, our son, came into his body more fully, the old one, the placenta, left this world. 🌿

The right time to let go

Jennifer VanLaanen-Smit

WHAT is Lotus Birth? It is when you do not cut the baby's umbilical cord from the placenta. You let it fall off when it is ready. Lotus Birth keeps the baby in seclusion for the first days of life. It helps the parents be patient at a time when they need to be. And it teaches trust, trust that our babies do indeed know the right time to let go of a part of their being no longer used.

The baby and the placenta arise from the same cell, so baby and placenta are one. Some say that when you leave the placenta attached, it results in a stronger immune system for the baby. All the life force of this organ gets transferred along the cord to the baby. When the cord falls off naturally, it slowly decreases the oxygen supply from the placenta to the baby. The women I've talked to give this birth a lot of spiritual weight. It takes a less 'violent' action and allows a natural transition.

A Lotus Birth slows the whole family down, letting the baby adjust to its new home; letting the baby be completely here and let go when the time is right for him or her.

It is reported that when the placenta is left intact, the baby is sensitive to having the cord or the placenta touched. Even when the baby is sleeping and the placenta is touched it can startle the baby. So there must be some feeling in the umbilical cord.

You can place the dry placenta in a cloth diaper. Salt down the placenta on both sides liberally. Tape the placenta up inside the diaper. It will drain a lot in the first few days. Change the diaper and re-salt once a day – more if needed. Keep the placenta dry and do not put anything around the cord stump. It will usually come away after three to seven days.

Or you can dry the placenta in a sieve, and place this into a larger bowl. This way air gets to all parts of the placenta to dry it quicker.

The placenta can start to smell, a kind of meaty smell. Light some incense if it bothers you. This will only last a day or two, sometimes not at all if the weather is warm and dry.

Eisa, a midwife, says: 'I learned that the placenta is best left for at least two-and-a-half hours to complete central nervous system communication. One couple I worked with allowed it to remain uncut for nearly 24 hours and felt good about giving it a final snip when it became too brittle to move the baby without causing tugging that concerned them. What I'm learning is that if it's cut before the two-and-a-half hour mark the baby responds by crying. LET IT BE . . . THAT'S MY COUNSEL! The last birth I attended a few nights ago, the parents left it uncut for about an hour and the baby definitely responded when it was cut.'

Donna Losoya from Gentlebirth has this to say about Lotus Birth: 'I have read that a particular Aboriginal tribe practises non-severance of the cord and just carry the placenta along with the newborn child until the baby's body discards it. They speak telepathically in their tribe, and I have to say they are the most gentle and in-tune people as a group. Then there are vegetarian monkeys, also a very gentle species, who do the same.

'I have read that the baby and the placenta grow from the same cell and they share the same aura. Aura is the etheric body surrounding everything that has matter and can be seen with the human eye. The 'glow' in pregnancy is a good example. It is quite a beautiful experience to know babies are born with the ability to sense people's moods. Everyone's aura colours have specific indications of their wellbeing and their mood.

'The placenta can be looked at as a limb that dies and it is a bodily extension for the baby. Instead of cutting away a body part that is almost useless in the physical form, we can give the baby the personal time (on a spiritual level) to let go of its life supply that has taken care of him or her during the in-womb existence, giving the baby the space (on a spiritual level) to decide when it isn't needed any more.

'The placenta should be left in a strainer the first 24 hours until the Whorton's jelly is gone, then the placenta can be washed and liberally salted on both sides and kept in a beautiful hand-made bag with a couple of cloth diapers catching drainage inside this bag. Then just rest it on the baby's abdomen; they don't mind being close to it and neither should the mother – it's a body part for her as well. Then wrap the baby in a blanket with the placenta inside for visitors who come by – if you desire visitors. Washing and salting each morning and night will help the process along quickly.

'If haemorrhage occurs, take a swift bite of the placenta – it has blood-clotting abilities for the mother!'

Chapter 8

Parents' stories

A child is born naturally, the hygienic way

Naomi Hermann

WHEN I learned that I was pregnant I wanted my child to have the best start in life possible. I already knew about Natural Hygiene and knew it would provide the baby with that kind of start to life.

My parents had been into health and what they taught all seven of their children made sense. In 1981 I even had worked for a while with Dr Ralph Cinque at Utopia Health Centre, Yorktown, Texas. That gave me a chance to see that what we have been taught really worked.

Two of my brothers had worked at the California Health Sanctuary in Hollister, California. I was living nearby in Stockton and was lucky enough to be accepted on the Sanctuary staff during most of my pregnancy. Living there gave me a chance to get fresh air and sunshine and to have the most ideal diet possible for myself and for my baby. It was a diet made up of raw fruits, nuts and seeds, and vegetables that grow above the ground. My work kept me active and busy. I made it a point to get some exercise on a regular basis. I felt good throughout the whole nine months.

Early along the way I decided I didn't want to have my baby in a hospital. I wanted to have it in the most natural way possible and in surroundings where I felt comfortable. I decided to have it at home right there on the Sanctuary grounds, with friends present who knew me and cared about me. I just would not have felt right being in a strange place around strange people at such a personal time in my life.

About a month before delivery time I began attending weekly childbirth classes and learnt about proper breathing during labour.

The time arrives

On 27 January, a Thursday, I began feeling some slight cramping in my abdomen. It wasn't real to me that I might be starting in labour. I had plans to go shopping that day and really wanted to go to the movies that evening. Friends convinced me that it might be all right to go shopping, but that it would be a mistake to go to the show. I listened to what turned out to be good advice. I stayed home and went to bed early. The cramping continued and the contractions were fairly regular. They didn't hurt. It was just different, something I had never experienced before. I still couldn't really believe it was happening. But at about two in the morning I became convinced. The cramps had become contractions. There was no doubt about it; I was in labour. I called in three friends, other staff members, to be with me. One of them had been present during other birthings, which was reassuring for me. I admit to having thoughts go through my mind about the wisdom of my decision to have a home birth. Only it was too late to change plans now.

The real labour set in a little after 4.00 a.m. At the time it seemed to hurt, but no so bad that I had to cry out. Later I realised that what I thought to have been pain really wasn't so bad and that most likely it came from my not knowing what to expect and tensing up. I know already that next time it will be a lot easier because I will know what to expect.

All in all, time passed quickly and at 8.30 a.m. in the morning, Friday 28 January 1983, Natalie Grace Hermann came into the world. She weighed 6 pounds, 14 ounces and was 17.5 inches long.

It was interesting that my water never broke. The bag was intentionally ruptured after the head had totally emerged. I did not even have a little bit of fear. It is hard to describe the sense of joy, peace, elation and fulfilment I felt immediately after the baby was born and was laid upon my breast. The placenta came out easily a couple of minutes later.

We did not wash the baby. We left her just as she came out. She was covered with what seemed to me to be a white salve. It was creamy and seemed to be there intentionally and for a purpose, like a protection for her skin exposed to its new air environment for the first time. We left it on. And it was amazing to see it disappear by itself within one day, as if it either evaporated or soaked in. She was clean without having been bathed and her skin was soft and glowing.

We did another thing different from any birth I ever had heard about up until a few months before my own baby was born. We did not cut the cord and discard the placenta. It is called 'birthing whole' or 'lotus birthing'. We had read about this in *Naturally, The Hygienic Way* (Sept 1982). We wrapped the placenta in gauze, then in a towel. The cord continued to connect the baby to the placenta. It seemed different, even strange, because we were going against all tradition. However, it really wasn't a bother.

It was interesting to watch the change in the cord. You could almost see the changes in it hour by hour. Then, only two-and-a-half days later, the cord fell away from the navel. That's all there was to it.

I hadn't had a lot of experience with newborn babies. But I can tell you that Natalie was the most peaceful, contented baby I ever had seen. She still is to this day. I can't positively say that she is this way because of her being birthed whole. At the same time, it ended up the way the 'birthing whole' literature said it would.

How I felt afterwards

It seems important to mention how I felt physically after the delivery. I felt great! I wasn't exhausted or tired. I was strong and had lots of energy. And it wasn't stimulation from the excitement of the birth. There was no let-down. There never has been. I felt good enough to have gone right back to work if I had needed to. I didn't for a few days, but that same day around noon I stood at the sink and shampooed my hair.

If by 'labour' people mean hard work, having my baby wasn't hard work at all. It left me feeling fine. And I feel that if we were really healthy people it would be even easier than it was for me. Being pregnant isn't having a disease and having a baby shouldn't be at all painful. It should be a pleasant and joyful experience.

Natalie Grace is two-and-a-half months old now. She is gaining weight steadily on a totally natural diet of her own mother's milk. My body seems to make all she needs out of the foods I eat. These are the same foods I ate before she was born – fruits, nuts and seeds, and vegetables that grow above the ground. I eat these foods raw.

Natalie is a happy, smiling, laughing child most of the time. She gets a lot of love and affection, not just from me but from all the people around her.

The whole experience of motherhood, including the pregnancy, has made me a more serious, thoughtful person. I want to be the best mother to my baby, and to other children I may have, that I possibly can be. Being a good parent is going to take a lot of learning and caring on my part. I see being a good parent as my most important responsibility and I am going to meet my responsibility.

In a few years I plan to have another child, and perhaps another after that. When I do, one thing is certain: I'll have them just as I had Natalie Grace – naturally, the hygienic way. ❧

The sacredness of birth

Anand Khushi

WHEN I first heard of Lotus Birth, I knew that this was how babies could be born gently and whole. It seemed so perfect that I knew that this was the birth I wanted for my baby. I am fortunate to live at the place where Australia's first Lotus Birth took place, and the pathway had already been cut.

My partner and I began preparation for a Lotus Birth by asking our friends for their stories – how had they cared for the placenta, how did it feel, how long did it take. As with a labour, each experience was unique and seemed to evolve. Mischa suggested salting the placenta – he is a chef – to preserve it. We were concerned about it going off in the heat before the baby had let go of it. I made a beautiful placenta bag – my first sewing creation! – in which to store it.

Aswan Liam Shankara was born into warm water in a beautiful round room, with six amazing women around holding the space and assisting my partner and me. It was a blessed beginning for this wondrous new being. The labour had been scary at times, but was mostly ecstatic and problem-free. It was an incredible journey

inwards, meeting myself and my baby, but also a journey outwards
into the cosmos.

Aswan's placenta arrived about twenty minutes after he did,
it dropped out as I stood up. Luckily the cord was quite long so
that the placenta could be scooped up while the baby was held. I
watched as the placenta was placed in a colander to drain. Another
small cord was also attached to the placenta. Aswan cried if anyone
except his father touched the placenta or the cord; he seemed to be
very aware of it. The cord appeared very beautiful to me; I loved
looking at it and watching it over the coming days as it dried up.
The placenta was covered in salt, and Mischa, wonderful in his
devoted care, changed the salt each day.

At first it was awkward to nurse Aswan with the large bowl
attached, but after a couple of days the placenta had reduced enough
to fit into a smaller bowl, which Mischa wrapped up. I was surprised
that I felt quite detached from the placenta and its care, but I was
busy with my new role as mother. Mischa would wax lyrical about
the placenta smelling so much like goose livers, 'delicious'! I squirted
milk on Aswan's navel when it was red, but this seemed normal.
After five days and a five-hour cry, Aswan let go of his placenta.

The time Aswan spent joined to the placenta was a healing
time for me, and something about his stillness and wholeness had a
big impact on me. I had never seen anyone so much 'in' their body,
with movements so precise and elegant. I felt a deep satisfaction
holding him on my belly while his cord was still attached, and an
ache seemed to depart. Yet, it was six months before my partner and
I let go of the placenta and planted it under a fig tree – still wrapped
up and with the cord attached. The Lotus Birth, with its time of
movement limitation and its evocation of sacred ritual, awoke in
me the sacredness of birth, at the same time making the transition
for this new being to come among us as gentle and welcoming
as possible.

A sacred rite of passage

Kairava Deva Shan-Ra

OUR son, Anu Shan-Ra, was water-born 20 March 1992, gently and in his own good time, into the arms of his father. The birth itself was a powerful, transformative process with its own organic rhythm and expression, and I had to keep letting go – trusting and surrendering to forces that were way beyond my comprehension. Anu knew how to be born, my body knew how to give birth – all I could do was SURRENDER! For me, this is the signature of a Lotus Birth – surrender. We were well prepared for the after-care of the placenta, yet the journey was deeply unknown . . . the answers to our questions: 'why?', 'how will it be?' were all in the realm of the unknown.

Once Anu and his placenta had been born, his placenta was placed in a bowl. He had a relatively short cord, so we had to keep the bowl as close to him as possible. He was aware of his placenta, so contact with it was kept to a minimum. This is a most precious time for mother and babe to commune – we were all very aware of the vulnerability of new life.

I'd like to elaborate on the after-care of the placenta, because once that is established, one can enjoy the magic of the coming days. A few hours after the birth, we bathed and drained the placenta in a colander, then, twenty-four hours later, placed it, well covered, in a bowl of sea salt. The salt is an excellent preservative and drying medium. We then daily changed the sea salt. His cord started drying after twenty-four hours, and within two days was quite brittle. Once it had dried up to his navel, we gave him a daily sea salt bath, because his navel was tender and irritated by any kicks pulling at his cord. Caring for the cord and placenta was very simple. Looking back, it seemed a welcome rite to perform practical tasks in the first days of life, which were new to us all.

Anu was very 'other-worldly' in those days of transition, and would lie so still in my arms or on the bed. He seemed so complete, and I would sit and absorb this new being . . . soak in his smell, in his stillness, and fall in love. There was nothing to do – Kushala, my partner, took care of washing nappies; friends brought us meals. I know now that Lotus Birth is a sacred rite of passage – an honouring of mother and babe, and an honouring of new life: so precious. It would seem as though his being in its fullness was descending, and as that happened, I found I could let go of any incompleteness in my own birth experience. Anu let go of his cord after six days, ready to receive the world.

The wonder of Lotus Birth

Simone Lukacs

ABOUT eight years ago I first heard about the practice of Lotus Birth. Something resonated within me, and when I fell pregnant a short time later I knew deep down that this was the way I wanted my baby to come into the world. It seemed the natural choice. The only choice. My partner and I have not for one second regretted making that decision. In fact, it has been a decision that has shaped not only our two children's lives, but our own lives as well, in many incredible and wonderful ways.

The physical aspects of caring for the baby, umbilicus and placenta were very, very easy. As Seireadan was born in the middle of summer we thought it best to salt the placenta. First we drained it in a colander set in a basin for about 24 hours. After that we put it in a salt-lined bowl and covered it with more salt. The bowl was then simply wrapped in a nappy. We changed the salt daily for eight days. At the precise moment Seireadan decided to let go, he simply did. It was beautiful.

We were overwhelmed by the calmness of our newborn baby. He was so dreamy and soft, yet so very aware of what was happening around him. We were especially overawed by the attention he paid his placenta and his father Steve, as Steve cared for the placenta each day.

Second time around there was not a moment of hesitation. We definitely wanted this baby to experience Lotus Birth. And while some aspects were similar, it was quite a different experience. Madeleine decided she only wanted to hold on to her placenta for four days. She kicked and wriggled so much more than her big brother and actually gave it the final yank herself.

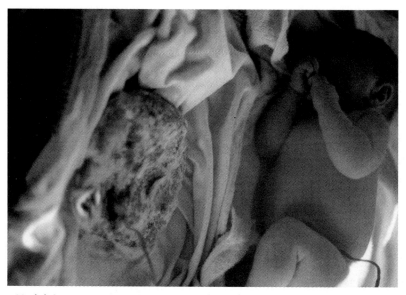

Madeleine   Photo: Simone Lukacs

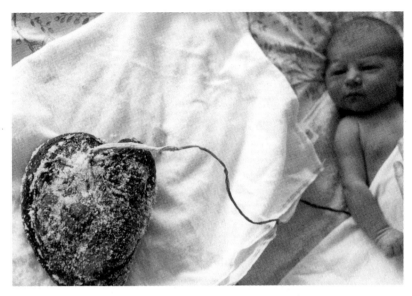

Seireadan's heart-shaped placenta   Photo: Simone Lukacs

It is said that because the baby chooses to let go of the placenta when he or she truly wants to, there is no hole or weakness in the auric field. The aura of a Lotus Birth baby is complete (as opposed to that of a person whose cord has been cut, often violently). This complete energetic field in turn leads to a more whole and robust physical immune system. I can attest to this argument one hundred per cent. Both Seireadan and Madeleine have never been to the doctor for illness, never had an ear or chest infection, never caught a communicable disease such as chicken pox. If they've ever injured themselves, they healed very fast and well.

With few reference points to 'know' whether Lotus Birth was the right thing for our children, my partner and I 'felt' it was the right thing to do. And over the last six-and-a-half years it keeps feeling right. That gentle, whole beginning to life has allowed our children, at least from my viewpoint, to be the human beings that they came here to be. They are resolute, definite, solid, enthusiastic, clear – and don't seem to let life dish up 'no' for an answer. Both in their own unique way, they feel confident expressing themselves. Something in their eyes, in the way they look at people, look through people, tells me they have manifested Spirit as wholly and beautifully as possible.

Not once did the placenta get smelly or unpleasant. Not for the eight days in summer with our first-born, nor four days in winter with our second babe. I'm sure the salting helped. But mostly I think it was the sacredness of the event. Seireadan's placenta even dried into the shape of a heart.

A friendly warning: choose Lotus Birth only if you have accepted the idea of being truly challenged by your children on a daily basis. Nothing escapes them. As a parent you will be able to get away with little. They will expect nothing but the highest personal integrity from you. But it will be repaid trillion-fold, because the crystalline radiance of a lotus-born child is truly magnificent to behold. Our children, and Lotus Birth, have been gifts. We truly recommend it.

A whole experience

Nine months before conception
a brilliant blue circle of light
appeared before me,
glowing luminously,
watching quietly.
I knew it was the child
that would be born to me.
My body ripened,
and in the swirl
and tenderness
and passion of union
he came to me.

I felt his presence
and welcomed it
with all my heart.
It was he who chose
a Lotus Birth.
He very strongly, very directly
let me know
that was what he wanted.
It was the easiest decision to make.
My entire body,
mind and spirit
knew what a whole experience
it would be
for both of us.
And it was.
Nine months went past,
my belly swelling
so round.
He kept telling me things,
wise things,
when I needed to hear them most.
And then, one hot, hot summer night
after making love
in the full moon light,
he decided it was time.
The waves were soft at first,
becoming stronger,
then so big they moved the earth
beneath me.
The full moon
as my witness,
with loved ones all around,
I laboured through the night.
And in the freshness
of the morning
my son began to appear
from between my legs.

Just a few minutes later
he slithered out,
ever, ever so gently.
And there,
in front of us, a baby boy,
a perfect being.
A soul of such magnitude and peace
I felt as though
I had given birth
to the first baby
on the first day.
Soon my legs began to quiver
and the placenta appeared,
big and red and round.
It was beautiful,
never had I seen
anything like it before.
For the next eight days
it protected my son,
let him enter the earth
gently,
innocently,
completely,
slowly drying out
till he needed it no longer.
It was a test of patience
for me, not him,
and in the fullness of the moment
he let go,
eyes open,
fully aware,
completely present.
Now, at nine months old
he is still totally present
in all he does,
reaching out into the world
with so much enthusiasm and delight.

He is a Wise One.
I watch him look
into people's eyes,
into their souls,
with all the wisdom
of an Ancient.

Simone Lukacs

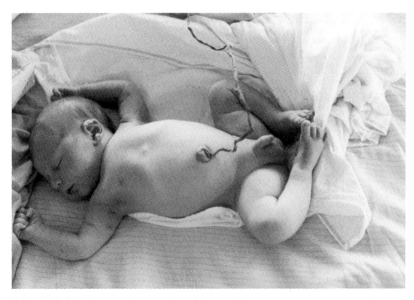

Seireadan   Photo: Simone Lukacs

Allowing completion

Karyn Patterson

TALKING with friends and reading articles about Lotus Birth stirred something within me. Then I witnessed the birthing of a baby and its placenta and was stirred even more deeply as the mother placed them together ever so gently, saying that she didn't want to cut the cord. I knew then that was what I wanted to do when the baby growing inside me was born.

Four weeks later Raphael emerged. When his placenta followed soon after him, there was such a stillness in the room – there wasn't anything more to be done except to celebrate this life together. We had his placenta in a bowl for the rest of the day. Come evening, we towel-dried and lightly salted it, wrapped it in a nappy, and placed it inside a lotus bag I had enjoyed sewing during my pregnancy. The next day the cord became brittle, and out of concern for it pulling where it joined Raphael we moved them as little as possible. I didn't salt it any more – its aroma stayed that of a newborn puppy.

Raphael's brother, sister and dad took good care of us, and we never left each other's side in the four days the placenta took to come away. Around the time of separation, when we were both dozing, I felt a lot of sensation in my belly, with a strong sense of something leaving me. I thought, 'Yes, allowing the placenta and baby to separate in their own time is allowing for the continuation and completion of a process I didn't fully understand'.

I feel an extra specialness with Raphael, who is now two – a love that previously I had only imagined possible. From the beginning of our journey together, there were many things that were different from the journeys of our other two children – but the Lotus Birth greatly enriched how we feel about each other.

Lotus Birth: a ritual for our times

Dr Sarah Buckley

'When I was a baby in your tummy, there was this love-heart
thing . . . I'll draw it for you . . . it's not the placenta. When
I was born the cord went off the love-heart thing and onto
there (x).'

Zoe Lennox Buckley, aged 5
lotus-born

Making the choice

I HAVE experienced Lotus Birth with both my second and third children, after being drawn to it during my second pregnancy through my contact with Shivam Rachana at the Centre for Human Transformation in Yarra Glen near Melbourne. Lotus Birth made sense to me at this time, as I remembered my time training in GP obstetrics and the strange and uncomfortable feeling of cutting through the gristly, fleshy cord that connects baby to placenta and mother. The feeling for me was somewhat like cutting through a boneless toe and I was happy to avoid this cutting with my coming baby. Through the Centre I spoke with women who had chosen this option for their babies. Some had experienced a beautiful postnatal time and felt a heightened awareness of their baby's individuality. Some women also described their Lotus-Birth child's self-possession and completeness. Others described it as a challenge, practically and emotionally. Nicholas, my partner, was concerned

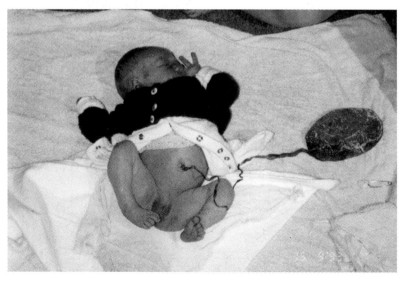

Zoe Photo: Sarah Buckley

that it might interfere with the magic of those early days, but was happy to go along with my wishes.

The practicalities

Zoe, our second child, was born at home on 10 September 1993. Her placenta was an unusual oval shape, which was perfect for the red velvet placenta bag which I had sewn. Soon after the birth, we wrapped her placenta in a cloth nappy, then in the placenta bag, and bundled it up with her in a shawl that enveloped them both. Every 24 hours, we attended to the placenta by patting it dry, coating it liberally with salt, and dropping a little lavender oil onto it. Emma, who was two, was keen to be involved in the care of her sister's placenta.

As the days passed, Zoe's cord dried from the umbilical end, and became thin and brittle. It developed a convenient 90-degree kink where it threaded through her clothes, and so did not rub or irritate her. The placenta, too, dried and shrivelled due to our salt treatment, and developed a slightly meaty smell, which interested our cat! The cord separated on the sixth day, without any fuss; other babies have cried inconsolably or held their cord tightly before it separated.

Our third child, Jacob Patrick, was born on 25 September 1995, at home into water, with his sisters Emma (four) and Zoe (two) present to welcome him. We needed a way to float the placentas, as I wanted to stay immersed with Jacob afterwards, and so we used an ice cream carton with a corner cut away for the cord. Zoe and Emma joined us in the tub, which water-logged the placenta as they splashed around and sang to Jacob. This time, we put his placenta in a sieve to drain for the first day. As with Zoe, we cared for Jacob's placenta by daily drying, salting and sprinkling it with lavender oil; we then wrapped it in a cloth nappy inside the red velvet bag which I had made for Zoe. This was mandolin-shaped, with Velcro down one edge to open it, and it enveloped the cord as well as the placenta.

I felt very cocooned in these early days with Jacob, and hardly moved him from the bed. I didn't encourage others to hold him, and I didn't dress him, but wrapped nappies and coverings around him. It felt good to not be fiddling with clothing at this time. His placenta was bundled up beside him like a twin.

This Lotus time was an immensely enriching time for me, as it allowed Jacob and myself to be quiet and unencumbered. I stayed

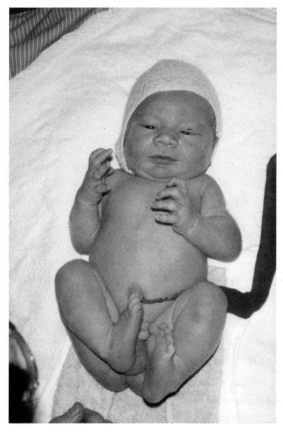

Jacob   Photo: Sarah Buckley

in a still space with him, while Nicholas cared for Emma and Zoe. I feel that it nourished all of our family and helped us to adjust to Jacob's arrival with ease and grace.

Jacob's cord separated in just under four days, and I feel that he drank deeply of the stillness of that time. His short 'breaking forth' time was perfect also because my parents arrived from New Zealand the following day to help with our household.

The aftermath

Lotus Birth was a beautiful ritual which enhanced the magic of the early days with our babies. I notice a self-possession and integrity with my lotus-born children and I also believe that the cohesiveness of our family unit is due, at least in part, to the imprint of unity and non-separation that comes from Lotus Birth.

The red velvet bag I made for Zoe's placenta has since been used by other parents for 20 Lotus-Birth babies.

The ripe pear

Davini Joy

MY second child, Zak Walter Malcolm, was born on 23 July 1996. I had a deliciously delicate start with this birth for about thirty hours, prior to starting full labour. I had gentle and painless hindwater leak; a slow dripping of the magical fluid that had cushioned my son while he grew inside me. It was my first outward contact with my child. I felt like a big juicy pear completely ripe and ready.

I spent the day preparing myself and dropping into the stillness, enjoying my final day as a mother of one. Satchi, my first son, had been born four years earlier – a Lotus Birth at home in water, and I hoped for the same again. Sometime during the afternoon my first-born hugged me and said: 'I'm a bit teary, mum, but I'm ready for this baby to be born now'. I felt my heart open deeply to my darling Satchi and to my new child; I felt the expansion into being a mother of two. It was different to being a mother of one. At age thirty-five I experienced the richness and maturing of myself as woman and mother.

My partner Peter took the day off work and prepared himself. I loved knowing that he was nearby. My midwife and dear friend, Jenny Teskey, popped in for a cuddle. I felt loved. I felt surrendered. I couldn't sleep much that night – I was ready. It was during the Olympics and I watched Kieren Perkins swim his 1,500 m heat, and fairly soon afterwards a warm gush came and my labour commenced. It was about 2.30 a.m. My birth team of Jenny, Sunderai, Kairava and Caroline joined us. It was very peaceful. My cervix was opening easily; my body was doing well.

Satchi and Zak   Photo: Davini Joy

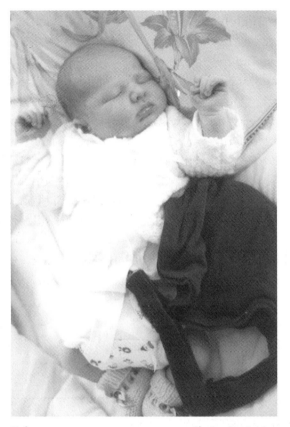

Zak   Photo: Davini Joy

At one stage a small amount of cord slipped through my cervix. My midwives and Peter felt that I should transfer to hospital. It was the last thing I wanted. I checked with my inner knowing – a voice that I have grown to trust deeply – and she said, 'go, surrender and all will be well'. So surrender I did, and off we went to the local hospital. Kairava stayed at home to watch over sleeping Satchi.

It was a 'head down, bottom up' trip for me. Miraculously the car trip sorted everything out – the doctor announcing that he could only feel my cervix and that the cord had gone back into my uterus. I could go home again if I wanted to. We had been at the hospital for all of twenty minutes; my cervix was dilating quickly. It took a fair amount of energy to contemplate the trip home, but I knew that I wanted a Lotus Birth and I knew that I wanted to be home, so after a quick vomit off we went. It was dawn; Venus, the morning star, was in the sky; there was a glow on the horizon. At that point I knew that my child was coming soon. I was glad to be sitting in the car, taking in the land.

We arrived home at 7 a.m. I had my final contraction in the garden, came inside and got into our birth tub. Wonderful warm water soothed my body as I relaxed and felt the stillness of transition. The urge to push commenced soon after. Satchi woke up and wandered in, and our beautiful Zak appeared at 7.24 a.m. He was born into the water and spent about a minute under water stretching his body and looking about. During this time, Jenny checked his heartbeat and pulsating cord. The placenta was still providing all the oxygen he needed, as it had done in utero. I felt the impulse to bring Zak up for his first breath, which I did with Peter's help. As I cuddled him to my left breast, I felt Zak's body charge with this first breath. I saw and felt a gentle electric quiver move through him. What a gorgeous pink baby he was.

We stayed in the tub for a while and thirty minutes later, once on dry land, I birthed Zak's placenta into a bowl. The cord remained intact. The placenta felt soothing and gentle as it came out. For a while, we strained the placenta in a sieve over a bowl, and then wrapped it in a cloth nappy and put it in a red velvet placenta bag lent to us by our friend, Dr Sarah Buckley, who had used it for the births of two of her babies. After twenty-four hours we put lavender oil and sea salt on the placenta and changed the nappy daily, adding a little more salt and lavender oil. I loved the fact that this placenta bag had a history – Sarah had passed it on to a number of women before me and in turn it has moved on to others since. What shared sisterhood! I recommend the use of a placenta bag. It is soft to cuddle up with and can easily be wrapped up with the baby.

In the next couple of days we hung out with our very peaceful Zak and his placenta. I remember snuggling up for a sleep with my hand on the bag. I felt a pulsating similar to a heartbeat coming from the placenta – it moved through my body, through Zak's, and through itself. I felt a circle of energy between the three of us and luxuriated in this magic for a long time. It fed me a deep richness and rest that I find difficult to convey in words.

Zak's cord came off nearly three days after birth in the still of the night as he slept on Peter's chest. The birth felt so complete. I am blessed to have had my children this way.

Ela-rose

Katrina Japp

I MET my daughter on Valentine's Day, the morning after a dramatic thunderstorm: a rose pink billowing sunset and an almost full moon set the scene. For the past six months I had been in a kind of protracted early labour, following the passing over of my beloved, my children's father. It was a time of extraordinary pain; of letting go once precious ideals of family, a country home and a tantric union; of facing my death urges and strengthening my life urges; of surrendering and trusting spirit far beyond anything imagined. It was a time of blessings as a web of invisible but tangible love and strength was spun around me by precious, precious friends.

Early on her birth day, I awoke to meditate and invite the being within to join me in this world as I was now ready for the journey forth. She slipped easily into my hands and into this world

– an extraordinary gift; another embodiment of the love Barry and I share – Ela-rose, which means 'all, entirely love and beauty'.

I hung onto an apple tree, which stands outside the temple of the Centre for Human Transformation. My three-year old son Jasha climbed and swung from the branches as expansions swept through me. Rachana was my anchor. I knelt on all fours on Mother Earth as the pain became all of me and more. Then I decided flies, grass and meconium don't mix, so I went into the temple, where my handmaiden Khushi had made preparations. Ignoring these and unsure of what my body wanted to do, I knelt next to the almost empty water bath and clutched the rim. During the second explosive, excruciating push, I was taken totally by surprise to feel the baby's head in my hands between my legs. She slithered out, and Rachana helped me to move her into a position which enabled her to start breathing. She was all purple and green, her nose and mouth thick with meconium, but she wasn't stressed and she started breathing without any difficulties. I feel she released the meconium to initiate my 'fight–flight' response for a speedy delivery, perhaps because I had been in so much pain for so long.

My son and his support person, my brother, arrived before the placenta. My midwife, Ally, was also with us. I was still uncertain about a Lotus Birth, even after the placenta slipped out revealing an elegant, long, thin, translucent, white and blue cord – perfect for a Lotus Birth. I had it in mind to cut the cord at some stage, if the placenta started to smell or became difficult to manage. All the babies born at the Centre were Lotus Births, so I thought I should 'keep up with the Shan-Ras' and follow tradition, without actually appreciating the essence of the practice.

The placenta drained in a colander for thirty-six hours. As we washed and drained it, Rachana spoke to Ela about what we were doing. I noticed how this amazing little being responded when her placenta was handled. As this awareness grew, I realised that this was Ela-rose's placenta and the decision to part with it was hers, not mine. It was frustrating not to be able to snuggle as closely to her body as I would have loved to do. She slept most of the time and I fed her lying down. Bringing up wind required delicate handling as the cord dried out and pulled uncomfortably at times. We had a bath together with her placenta in its container high and dry. Ela blissed out in my arms. When the placenta got in my way, I had to remind myself to respect my daughter's decision and timing, which was good practice for our dance to come. I finally came to liking it – almost – as it lay there in between us.

On the fourth night, she was uncharacteristically unsettled. I said to her that if she wanted me to cuddle her more fully, she needed to let go of her placenta. The next morning, Jasha woke up and went around to Ela's side. He'd been calling her 'brother or sister', as we named her in utero. He began his 'dance of joy' on his toes, arms out and moving side to side in time with his head. 'Hooray', he said, 'I've got a sister'. Ela was much more in her body. She had been so still, and now startled more easily and slept less. She felt present for longer periods. She had landed ever so gracefully.

Those five days were so special, so perfect for me and my children. I drank in the surroundings – its colours, sounds and moods. Our bodies and souls were nourished by the community members, who tended us with love. I am very thankful that such a safe space was created for us. I look now at my white-haired child, who's doing a wonderful impersonation of a Beluga whale calf. She has her 'empty lap' radar turned on all the time, and sits quite happily on anyone's knee, blissfully radiating peace, love and light.

Ela-rose's placenta is one of my sacred objects. It was the last part of Barry's physical being inside me. If Ela agrees, and after she's taken it to school for 'show and tell', I would like to plant it under a rose bush with some of Barry's ashes. That should really kick the blooms along.

Zephyr

Christal

THERE were many friends present at the time of my delivery. So much energy was welcoming the new being and helping me as well. It is all stored in my brain as one of the most fulfilling and rewarding things to ever have happened to me. My son Zephyr Aaron (gentle wind – lofty and inspired) was born 30 August 1975, at 11.45 p.m. His cord was not cut, and the placenta was cured in the upper third of a pyramid and also in sunlight after coming away from the child.

When I had been in doubt about Lotus Birth dealing with pyramids, I consulted with a very special friend, and he readily explained the functions of pyramids, thus giving my husband faith enough to build one. The pyramid was designed after the blueprint and we fixed it up beautifully. We put a candle on the very top of it and lit it every morning and evening before and after the birth.

Zephyr is just as you said he would be: full of peace; a complete circle, which has in turn extended my husband's as well as my aura. At first I thought that there was no reason why he seemed to be so beautiful and Christlike, except because he was my baby (the world's baby in truth) and that to other brothers and sisters he would not seem any different than any other baby. But this is not so! Everyone who beholds him exclaims over the peace that emanates from his being and how full and rich he is.

When I first gazed upon him I knew he had something more than other beings. A full aura! And now this blessed Aquarian age is indeed bringing people of wisdom who see the steps, hard and narrow, which will lead us back to the Sun Way. Zephyr, already being a perfect being from God, has taught me so much in so little time. I only pray I do everything possible to keep myself from laying my power trips on him and that he teaches me the pure way, as he is full and pure from the start!   🪷

Tristan's story

Trish Douglas

W HEN I first heard of Lotus Birth I was fascinated. At the same time I cringed because the idea seemed somewhat outlandish to me. However, in a rebirthing session I experienced my own cord being clamped and cut at birth. After that experience I decided to have a Lotus Birth for Tristan. My experience of this process was profound.

Labour was an awesome journey and after giving birth to Tristan the placenta came straight away with ease. The colours, texture, shape and smells were truly amazing. The placenta seemed to be of as much importance as the child itself.

Ecstasy filled the room for the whole time during which the placenta was connected. It was a beautiful thing; it kept John, myself and Tristan bound to each other. We first had the placenta in a cloth nappy, then in a bag I'd made. It was so easy, so natural and felt like a gift to our child and to ourselves, a sacred ritual. A dance. Tristan seemed to be in bliss.

The morning John had to go back to work, Tristan kicked off his cord with ease, as if to say, 'I'm here,' and a new journey began. To think back and remember the feeling of Tristan, whole, complete, lying there naked with his placenta, brings such joy to my heart. It was a very healing experience.   🪷

Ella Shiani

Branwen Hooke

I T was a cold, colourful May day when my daughter, Ella Shiani, swam head first from the waters of my womb into the birth pool in my bedroom. I had laboured all night, my mother beside me, breathing through each contraction, floating in the indescribable other world between them. I was awash with emotions. A baby. There was really going to be a baby. And I was going to be a mother. Nine months of preparations were at last coming to their frightening, exciting climax with an intensity that a million woman's stories could never have quite prepared me for.

I was encircled by a beautiful group of people, all completely supportive of my decision to have a lotus birth at home. What a blessing! I will be grateful to them all forever. The midwives with their infinite wisdom. My mother for her love, strength and belief in me. My younger sister for sharing her unashamed awe and affection. My doctor, who came in quietly, said 'you're doing beautifully,' and left me to it. Also to my stepfather and his mother, who held the outer circle, keeping us all warm and fed. My love and thanks go to them all. And of course my baby, who put it all in place.

Ella Shiani was born into the water, and as I lifted her up to the surface and held her tiny perfect body to mine I experienced deep peace. Bliss. The world as I knew it stood still. Time held its breath as we finally looked into each other's faces. So there you are little one. All soft and warm and wrinkled. Pinky purple, spotted white with vernix and topped by a sprinkling of hair. Oh precious, precious baby girl. In that moment there was nothing else, no one else in the whole world. Just us, and the love between mother and child. That moment will be with us forever, and it sent all my fears and doubts flying out the window.

I was helped out of the water and onto the bed, baby in arms, still joined to me by her umbilical cord. My eyes never left her as someone reminded me there was still the placenta to come out. I felt no urge to push anymore, so one of my team simply helped me to move from sitting to kneeling, and out it came. Such an amazing looking thing! I had never seen one before, and was struck by the bright blue 'tree' of veins. I remember thinking 'that is the tree of life'. My midwife asked permission and explained every step of the process to the baby as she patted dry and salted the placenta with organic sea salt. She wrapped it in a beautifully hand-made cotton placenta bag.

It was important to me that my baby be born in a gentle environment without intervention. Leaving the cord intact was a part of that process, and felt as natural to me as keeping her warm and offering my breast when she woke up hungry. I could not see with my eyes what function this amazing organ was performing, but I had a sense it was important. If the lungs know how to breathe and the heart knows how to beat, the placenta must know its job. Why interfere?

Now my gorgeous girl is one year old and learning to walk. Her confidence and obvious pleasure in life and learning are a joy to watch, and for me are a testimony to the wisdom and grace of natural birth.

A winter's child

Bodhi Priti

I HAD never really thought about or explored the subject of birth before, other than to say that I had been born. When I first heard about Lotus Birth, and listened to this totally new concept and the possibilities the birth process could hold, the words fell on me not unlike first experiences fall upon a newborn baby. They became an imprint and a map of future potential. When my partner and I were pregnant with our first daughter, Senie, it was clear to us that all being well, we would choose a Lotus Birth. I had prepared myself, as much as one can prepare for the unknown, with a great deal of bodywork and inner work, in the company of women experienced in these realms. My body swelled and her time inside me drew to a close.

It was a still winter's day, the day of her birth. I had gently laboured from morning till afternoon as I pottered around home, doing my final bit of nesting. The midwives arrived and as the evening settled in, so too did the labour. Shortly after I sank into the warm water of the tub, my waters broke and something like a tornado touched me. She came quickly, with a speed that was unexpected, and into the water she was born, into her father's hands . . . this beautiful perfect being.

I stood up a little while later and the full, red, blood-filled placenta slipped out. We caught it and placed it into a large ceramic bowl and with help, we left the tub.

Once warm and dry, the three of us lay together. The midwives faded into the background as our new family was cradled into the night. Senie slept, we watched and together, we melted into a deep stillness and silence that was to last three days. It was as if we were cocooned in a bubble and I felt myself being expanded to its very limits. Time stood still. As I look back now I see how full of reverence and sacredness it was, and yet so simple.

I have since come to see that one of the most striking qualities that I have noticed about Lotus Births is an absence of 'things to do'; less doing, more being.

During the time that Senie's cord was attached, our life was centred around the bed. We moved her very little, instead preferring to attend to her where she lay; I would often simply shift myself around to lie beside her and feed her on each breast. After the first twenty-four hours, the placenta had drained and we placed it on a bed of Celtic sea salt. By the end of the second day it had begun to dry out and the umbilical cord was quite stiff. On the third day she caught her cord between her toes and tugged at it, as she had done a day earlier when I anxiously moved to untangle it. This time I watched, aware that my anxiety was no doubt related to the loss of my own umbilical cord, and I breathed. The cord came away and the pink new skin of her belly button was revealed. A first cry emerged as her lips and mouth were searching. Out of the stillness she came, with a large voice and a voracious appetite.

Chapter 9

Midwives' experiences with Lotus Birth

Attentiveness and patience

Sunderai Felich

MY first experience of Lotus Birth was in 1986 when Tika was born. I went to visit the day after her birth. I knew that Kushna, her mother, had chosen to have a Lotus Birth, and I was very interested to know what that entailed. When I arrived at the bedroom door I could go no further – I felt that going any closer was tantamout to intruding on a very sacred space.

I am working as a childbirth educator and a doula. A doula is a woman who provides physical, emotional and informational support to women and their families before, during and after childbirth. I have had the privilege of attending over twenty Lotus Births. (Independent Midwife Jenny Teskey has attended 28 Lotus Births since 1992.)

One of the Lotus Births I observed over several days was the birth of Kian. His parents Maria and Ross were looking forward to having a Lotus Birth. Maria talked of it as 'a sacred time of transition from the protection of the placenta to the protection of the mother's sheath', anticipating a pleasurable experience.

However, three days after the birth, Maria's nipples were sore, Kian's nappy kept falling off, and the cord was constantly in the way. This turn of events severely tested Maria's patience.

'We both almost reached the point of wanting to cut the cord,' Maria told me. 'At this point Kian looked up and took one of our fingers in each hand. He looked at us for some time. He was so still. He then placed first one of his hands, then the other, onto his cord. And we understood. His cord stayed attached for another five days, until he was ready to let go.'

One important factor in following through with a Lotus Birth is attentiveness to the baby's wishes. Another quality that comes in handy at this time is patience. Understandably, many new parents are concerned about possible hazards, especially if they have not experienced a Lotus Birth before.

Salting the placenta   Photo: Davini Joy

Concerns that frequently arise are:
- Can I bathe the baby with the cord still attached?
- Is the redness around the navel okay?
- What if the navel gets infected?

Yes, you can bathe the baby – just have an extra person on hand to hold the placenta (in its container) out of the water.

Redness around the navel is normal and there have been no recorded cases of infection. If it does ooze a little around the navel, breast milk (which is full of vitamin E) will clear it up beautifully.

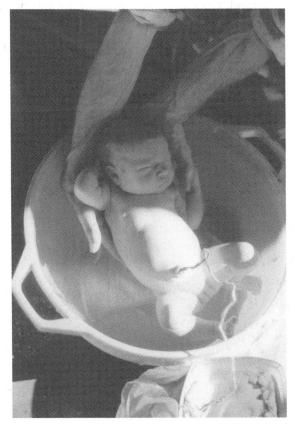

Bath with cord attached   Photo: Simone Lukacs

I strongly suggest that you do not wrap the placenta in anything plastic (plastic bag, disposable nappy). The placenta is alive. It is fulfilling its function until the cord comes away at the navel.

At one birth I attended the placenta was wrapped in a plastic bag. By the following day it was very 'on the nose' and had started to fall apart. The cord then had to be cut.

Most births I attend now are Lotus Births. I find it difficult to cut a cord. If I am asked to do so, I respect the parent's wishes, but suggest they find someone else to do it.

Care of the placenta
- Care of the placenta is a simple and straight-forward process that encourages stillness for mother and baby.
- After delivery of the placenta, it can be placed in a bowl. When ready, use a colander to drain off any excess blood and then place the placenta into the special bowl you have chosen for keeping the placenta. Often a ceramic bowl is used.
- You can leave the placenta in a bowl until the cord separates, or you can wrap it in a cloth nappy or gauze, or whatever material you choose. Some women make a beautiful round bag in which to keep the placenta, with a section that also covers the cord. This allows you to place the placenta next to the baby.
- It is important not to use plastic to wrap or cover the placenta, as then it cannot breathe and will become smelly.
- Leave the placenta for 24 hours before salting. Sea salt can be used to cover the placenta on top and underneath. How much salt is up to you. Not everyone chooses to salt the placenta.
- Salting of the placenta can be repeated each day for a few days, depending on how quickly the placenta dries out.
- In most cases the placenta will separate within four to seven days.

Clarity or subterfuge?

Anne Blanch

Dominic

FOR the five days after Dominic was born, as we waited for him to let go of his placenta, it felt to me as if we were all basking in quiet sunshine. The feeling of peace after his at times emotionally tumultuous pregnancy was replenishing – the calm before the storm, in fact. Dom's early babyhood was full of distress and pain, and looking back, those five days were like an oasis to be returned to and drunk from in the days and months to come.

Dom was born in front of the fire in the lounge room midafternoon in July 1993. Such a burst of pleasure for us all to see him! Bodhi had had a strong and at times uncomfortable labour, much of which was spent in the bath. Dom's third stage was completed easily within thirty minutes of his being born. His friends left the new family alone together and celebrated in traditional St Hilda's fashion with champagne on the back door step. This, however, was a mistake – the room was warm, and the placenta was not salted or cared for quickly enough. In the ensuing days its pervasive odour reminded us of our carelessness. We fought a rearguard action with washing, salt, Teatree oil and strong herbs.

Bodhi and Dom stayed in the lounge room at St Hilda's, which is the focal point of our house during winter. It was a wonderful and gentle time, being able to visit and sit with them at any time during the day or night. However, the days passed, the smell of Dom's placenta grew stronger, and I found that my impatience to get back to 'normal' grew as well. Finally, on day five, at the same hour he was born, he kicked at this cord, which parted with an audible 'ping', like a cork popping. We celebrated and cried again.

The process of being so intimately involved in a Lotus Birth was a profound experience for me. I found myself becoming so uncomfortable at times that I questioned whether it really was a safe process. However, Dom was always perfectly happy and content, and who can argue or interfere with that? I was left to confront my uncomfortable feelings around placentas, my potential manipulations to interfere with the fullness of process, and in the end, the total appropriateness of being.

Jade

Jade was born in the labour ward of the local maternity hospital. She was blessed with a sympathetic, if bemused, staff. Amanda had been transferred for failure to progress and had had an epidural for pain relief, but delivered otherwise without interventions. As their baby was born, Amanda and Kent unfroze and joy, relief and love flowed again. With such dynamic clarity moving, fulfilment of their wishes, however bizarre, was never in question.

The hospital's normal management of third stage involves oxytocin, controlled cord traction and the clamping of the cord within a few minutes of the baby's birth. So, no oxytocin was requested, a not unheard-of request; but then Amanda and Kent actually wanted to bundle up the placenta with the baby and not cut the cord, either then or later. The cord clamps, the scissors and bowls were all irrelevant. The doctor's and midwife's faces were a study. For a few moments their professional personas dropped, as did their jaws. Amanda and Kent were oblivious to all the fuss and the toing and froing that ensued. I'm sure they hardly heard instructions: that Jade's temperature needed to be taken four-hourly for forty-eight hours, and then two-hourly until the cord dropped off, as infection was 'inevitable'. For Amanda and Kent a Lotus Birth was a simple and unquestioned decision. For them it was the correct way, and the management of Lotus Birth was as easy as changing their baby's nappy.

I was at the hospital a lot around that time, and the staff questioned me closely about the outcome of Lotus Birth: what exactly happened, how long did it take, did any infection occur, why choose this option? However, despite this being a conservative hospital, I found only interest from those who were present at the birth. Such is the power of witness that comes into a place of clarity.

Sean

Unlike Amanda and Kent, whose clarity flew over the top of any objections, Tammy met opposition to a Lotus Birth with her second son, Sean. She worried over, but finally resisted, the opposition.

Tammy and David both have strong Catholic backgrounds. They live in a conservative community. David's chosen midwife was 'of the old school'. Tammy's relationship with her parents is strained.

Tammy had a fast and furious labour at home. She had told no-one of her family or friends that she was intending a home-birth. After Sean was born and Teresa, the midwife, was about to leave, David suggested that surely it was time to get rid of the placenta. Teresa, Tammy's chosen midwife, had not heard Tammy's weak mumble of assent and began talking about Lotus Birth. It was agreed that Sean's cord would be cut the next day during her post-natal visit. The instructions for this visit: 'take the scissors and cut the cord'. Tammy was clearly reluctant, so after leaving instructions about care of Sean's placenta, we left.

The next day the cards were finally on the table. Tammy wanted a Lotus Birth for her son. David found the concept so dis-gusting that he had difficulty holding Sean. To top it all off, the dreaded visit of the mother-in-law was imminent.

Tammy solved each issue, one by one. She declared that David simply had to put up with it. Tammy explained that to have these days exclusively with Sean was like being in a sea of sensual satisfaction, rocking to the different rhythm of his needs. Breastfeeding was easier than she had experienced with her first baby, and being with Sean allowed her time to change from work-mode to mother-mode.

The visit of her mother-in-law was solved by wrapping up the placenta and putting it inside the large jump suit, then wrapping baby and placenta in more blankets. Her mother-in-law was more intent on assessing Tammy's midwives' performance than on examining the baby closely, and merely thought Sean weighed a lot. This was explained with 'heavy bones'.

The placenta had a strong odour, increasing David's repugnance. Tammy, however, sailed on happily amid its wafts. In fact, she declared she liked the smell and would miss it when the placenta separated.

At no time did any of her family or friends know that Tammy had chosen a Lotus Birth, and they all believed her home birth occurred because of the speed of her labour.

Tammy's story provides an opportunity to appreciate the positive aspects of subterfuge, stubbornness and resistance. ❧

Midwifery and Lotus Birth consciousness

Kerry Radford

HAVING been interested in gentle birth choices for a long time, I learned about Lotus Birth at a workshop. I immediately felt that it was non-intrusive to the natural process but wondered about its specific significance. After listening to one woman's experience and reading the Lotus Birth manual, I became interested to learn more. My understanding of this gentle birth practice came about by being with Lotus Birth babies and sharing the experience of Lotus Birth with parents and siblings.

Over the following months I talked about the choice of Lotus Birth with several women planning home births. Some couples embraced it intuitively, whereas for others coming to this awareness was a gradual process. For some, Lotus Birth seems right, whereas for others it is not, and I respect their choice.

Friends of mine whose baby was due very soon knew that a Lotus Birth was what they and their baby wanted. The name they had chosen for her was Lotus, and I was privileged to visit them during the lotus time on the second day. The baby, with the placenta wrapped in a silk bag beside her, was very peaceful. The placenta was carefully looked after and I was amazed how hard and fine the cord was. I felt it to be a special time for the family – there was a sense of peace and joy in the home. Now I had talked with parents and observed a Lotus Birth, it was easy to share this with others.

My very dear friends chose a Lotus Birth for their daughter Matilda and asked me to make the placenta bag. Being able to share with them this experience and their insights was fascinating. I felt their love and respect for the placenta, and the significance this sacred process held for them.

At another birth the baby was born gently in water and was very calm and peaceful. The mother asked for the cord to be clamped. As the clamp was being placed on the cord, the baby cried and its breathing rate increased. When the parents saw the distress of their baby they asked for the clamp to be removed – their baby was resting quietly again. This baby had chosen a Lotus Birth.

At a pre-birth visit a couple readily embraced the Lotus Birth concept for their first birth. They had such trust in nature's process, and Lotus Birth meant a natural extension of this. To be in the presence of a Lotus Birth was a blessing for all involved. It allowed a gentle integration of the birth.

Another family had their second Lotus Birth experience. Their baby was very peaceful and the two older children showed great interest in the cord and placenta. Lotus Birth for them was an important step in the welcoming of their new sibling.

It is interesting to study various cultural practices that embrace both the physical and spiritual aspects of childbirth. These practices signify an acknowledgement of the placenta as a vital and respected organ. Lotus Birth reminds us of those sacred birth practices.

Being present at Lotus Births was a catalyst for the healing of my own birth trauma. Having observed the vital health and happiness of these Lotus Birth babies, I now have greater awareness and understanding of the natural process.

Longing for home

Jeannine Parvati Baker

A retained placenta

NANCY was American, Joe was English – yet they settled in Australia on account of his work. She was a relatively new Hygieia College student of mine, so when the phone rang one night, with Joe on the line sounding excited and with an overtone of concern about his wife, I was immediately attentive.

They had just given freebirth to a son and amidst their celebration for having an intimate and ecstatic home birth, the father was worried that the placenta hadn't come out yet.

'Well, how long is yet?' I asked.

'Several hours,' was his reply.

'How is the new mother doing?'

'OK at first, but as time went on, she became more unfocused and distant.'

'Was she bleeding?'

'Yes, but not too much.'

'Too much?'

The conversation went on like this for a little while, and then I spoke with the new mother herself.

Nancy sounded like the softest silk: smooth, as though in a wind tunnel, growing fainter for the white noise draping her voice. We talked about her exquisite new baby, their glorious birth, and her placenta. Then I invited her to look at how it served her to still have her baby's placenta – for when it no longer serves, the after-birth is released on its own accord.

I then talked to Joe and shared what I've noticed before when the afterbirth stays inside, close to the mother's heart, for many hours. The placenta is like the Museum of Eros – it is the primal tree of life and its fruit is the baby. The father's seed is what makes this tree possible and it is therefore connected to him. Fathers are awesome allies when it comes to bringing the harvest home.

What I didn't say to Joe was that in my observation, when a baby is born and all the attention goes from the mother to the newborn, some women hold their placentas. As a consequence, the focus soon shifts from the baby back to the mother – throw in a haemorrhage, and the mother may have more attention than she bargained for.

However, when a baby is freeborn, if a father immediately focuses on his wife or partner with gratitude, passion and love, as well as adores the new baby, she will more likely complete the birth with no drama. Therefore, I remind new fathers just who made this ecstasy possible and for him to show his gratitude to his lover (the

God-Self) – the mother of his new baby – and to do this sensually, for the senses are a gateway to spirit.

Later that night (and not all that much later), the phone rang again. This time Nancy's voice was strong and blessed with that tone of ascension – not unlike I imagine Inanna, the Babylonian Goddess, who went to hell and back with a smile.

Yes, she did ask her placenta and womb to dialogue, and she then understood her longing to be home – and what a profound metaphor this was! She missed the States and wanted to be rooted again on her home ground. But she had surrendered to what-is. Now that freebirth had turned her inside out, she felt a deep grief, and cried and cried as Joe held her close to him and she held the fruit of their loving, their baby, close to her heart. As she let go her feelings, Joe remarked, 'By the way, the placenta has come out'. They went on to experience their first Lotus Birth, keeping the original tree of life and new son as one.

Emotion = energy in motion

All the energy invested in repressing emotions, once released, can move mountains. Moreover, sobbing does apply fundal pressure. I have seen this often as a midwife – the more willing a new mother is to let her real feelings express to completion, the easier her placenta comes earthside. With Nancy and Joe their 'retained placenta' served to bring them even closer in trust. When I spoke one more time with Joe, his voice was in perfect resonance with Nancy's; they sounded like two Tibetan bells ringing.

As the placenta's function is somewhat sustained by breast-feeding, when a mother intends to fully nurse rather than wean the baby early (for any reason) the placenta is likewise 'in the flow'. In the freebirth shared above, the baby was weaned at six months due to an ideology. Later, when I visited the family in Australia, the baby at nine months was still complaining about the bottled meals and imposed bedtime and naps – again based on ideas of what is 'correct' according to a fashionable school of thought. In my mind, I link these two events – a placenta which wouldn't come out when all thought it 'should' and an early weaning based on dogma.

The tree of life (the placenta) is a source of mystery. When it stays for a while longer than people think it 'should', I wonder whether that is the God-Self talking? I have heard stories of 'retained placentas' coming out spontaneously up to a day or more after birth – even once while the postpartum mother was baking pancakes for the family the next day!

When I'm asked to validate how long any labor took, I categorically declare, 'nine months'. Labor, birth and afterbirth are essentially timeless events, and therefore from the perspective of this bigger picture, whenever a placenta happens to arrive is the right time.

Q: Can I bathe my baby with the cord and placenta still attached?
A: Yes. Bathe your baby as you normally would, simply keep the placenta nearby. It is best to have somebody hold the placenta as you bathe your baby, or it can float in an icecream container. It's okay if the cord gets wet, it will dry again.

Q: Can babies delivered by Caesarean have a Lotus Birth?
A: Yes – simply keep the placenta with the baby. There are examples of successful Lotus Births with Caesarean births.

Q: Can premature babies have a Lotus Birth?
A: Yes – they benefit greatly from keeping their placentas.

Shivam Rachana

Our babies - our teachers

Janet Ireland

FOR most parents the management of third stage of labour is not an issue, they have their babe in arms and are overwhelmed by the joy. However, for some individual families the handling and disposal of the placenta are of utmost importance.

The focus shifts from the mother's concentrated exertions to the miracle of the newborn. There is a sense of emotional and physical relief. During this sacred bonding time, the midwife does all she can to hold the space and stay open to parents' wishes.

In 1997, I retired from midwifery after working at the same institution in labour ward and birth centre for 22 years. I decided I had fought long enough and would devote my time to myself and my family. However, I had underestimated the powers of persuasion of pregnant women. Three months later I was heading to my first home birth. Everything was 'as usual', except I was now more able to respect parents' wishes than I had been in the hospital environment.

During a heat wave I was introduced to my first Lotus Birth. I had little confidence in our ability to prevent decomposition, if not infestation with flies, of the placenta. However, despite the soaring temperatures there was no problem with the placenta and the cord separated spontaneously on day five. The babe was very serene and I attributed this to the days of letting go of the placenta.

My eyes now open, I let subsequent clients know of their increased options in third stage. My practice had always been to deliver the placenta without cutting the cord, but now I paid more attention to this process. On one occasion after a beautiful water birth I went to cut the cord and was promptly stopped by the protests of the baby. This happened twice more and on the third try permission was granted in the form of silence! I firmly believe that our babies are our teachers.

Since that time I have attended 16 births where the parents requested Lotus Birth. ALL these babes have been well and thrived. There has been no difficulty with the diligent daily care of the placenta. Interestingly, of these births, six have been in hospital where the added benefits included that the mother and babe were not separated for routine hospital procedures. There have been no problems associated with Lotus Births that I have attended. Six of the families have cut the cord at various stages for various reasons. They said they felt 'it was time'. The record time for separation was nine days and the quickest three days.

In the practice of midwifery the midwife must remain open to the process and support the informed choices that parents make. When it comes to providing information to aid in that decision process, books like this will be a valuable resource.

References

Chapter 2

Lewis E Mehl, in Leslie Feher, *The Psychology of Birth,* Souvenir Press, London UK, 1980

Chapter 3

Beer A, Fetal erythrocytes in maternal circulation of 155 Rh-negative women, *Obstet Gynecol* 1969; 34,2:143–150

Botha M, Management of the umbilical cord during labour, *SA J Obstet Gynecol* 1968; August: 30–33

Brinsden P, Clark A, Post partum haemorrhage after induced and spontaneous labour *BMJ* 1978; ii: 855–856

Darwin E, *Zoonomia* Vol III 3ʳᵈ ed. London 1801:302

Doolittle J, Moritz C, *Obstet Gynecol* 1966; 27:529

Garrison R, Personal communication, 1999

Gartner L, Breastfeeding, breastmilk and the jaundiced baby, paper presented at *The Passage to Motherhood Conference*, CAPERS, Brisbane QLD, 1998

Gilbert L, Porter W, Brown V, Postpartum haemorrhage – a continuing problem, *Br J Obstet Gynaecol* 1987; 94:67–71

Grajeda R, Perez-Escamilla R, Dewey K, Delayed clamping of the umbilical cord improves hematologic status of Guatemalan infants at 2 mo of age, *Am J Clin Nutr* 1997; 65:425–431

Gunther M, The transfer of blood between baby and placenta in the minutes after birth, *Lancet* 1957; i:1277–1280

Hemminki E, Merilainen J, Long term effects of Cesarean section: ectopic pregnancies and placental problems, *Am J Obstet Gynecol* 1996; 174:1569–1574

Inch S, *Birth Rights: what every parent should know about childbirth in hospital*, Random House, New York NY, 1984

Jacobsen B, Perinatal origin of adult self-destructive behavior, *Acta Psychiatr Scand*, 1987; 76:364–371

Jacobsen B, Opiate addiction in adult offspring through possible imprinting after obstetric treatment, *BMJ* 1990; 301:1067–1070

Kinmond S, Aitchison T, Holland B, et al, Umbilical cord clamping and preterm infants: a randomised trial, *BMJ* 1993:306 (6871): 172–175

Landau D, Hyaline membrane formation in the newborn: hematogenic shock as a possible etiologic factor, *Missouri Med* 1953; 50:183

Lapido O, Management of the third stage of labour with particular reference to reduction of feto-maternal transfusion, *BMJ* 1971 18 March: 721–3

Linderkamp O, Placental transfusion: determinants and effects, *Clinics in Perinatology* 1982; 9:559–592

McKenzie I, Induction of labour and postpartum haemorrhage, *BMJ* 1979, 17 March: 750

Michaelson K, Milman N, Samuelson G, A longitudinal study of iron status in healthy Danish infants: effects of early iron status, growth velocity and dietary factors, *Acta Paediatr* 1995; 84:1035–1044

Morley G, Cord closure: can hasty clamping injure the newborn, *OBG Management* 1998; July: 29–36

Odent, Michel, *The Nature of Birth and Breastfeeding*, ACE Graphics, Sydney 1992

Odent, Michel, *Birth and Beyond*, Taped recording of a talk given at the Midwifery Today Conference, London, Sept 1998

Pearce, Joseph Chilton, *Evolution's End: Claiming the Potential of Our Intelligence*, Harper, San Francisco CA, 1992

Peltonen T, Placental transfusion: advantage and disadvantage, *Eur J Paediatr* 1981; 137:141–146

Prendiville WJ, Elbourne D, McDonald S, Active versus expectant management of the third stage of labour (Cochrane Review), in: *The Cochrane Library*, Issue 3, Update Software, Oxford 1999

Piscane A, Neonatal prevention of iron deficiency: placental transfusion is a cheap and physiological solution, (Editorial) *BMJ* 1996; 312(7024):136–137

Raine A, Brennan P, Mednick S, Birth complications combined with early maternal rejection at age 1 year predispose to violent crime at age 18 years, *Ach Gen Psych* 1994; 51:984–988

Rogers J, Wood J, McCandlish R, Ayers S, Truesdale A and Elbourne D, Active vs expectant management of the third stage of labour: the Hinchingbrooke randomised controlled trial, *Lancet* 1998; 351:693–699

Sorbe B, Active management of the third stage of labour: a comparison of oxytocin and ergometrine, *Obstet Gynecol*, 1978; 52,6:694–697

Usher R, Shepherd M, Lind J, The blood volume of the newborn infant and placental transfusion, *Acta Paediatr Scand* 1963; 52:497–512

Walsh S, Maternal effects of early and late clamping of the umbilical cord, *Lancet* 1968, 11 May: 997

Weinstein L, Farabow W, Gusdon J, Third stage of labor and transplacental hemmorrhage, *Obstet Gynecol* 1971; 37, 1:90–93

World Health Organization, *Care in Normal Birth: a practical guide*, World Health Organization, Geneva, 1996

Chapter 4

Anne Deveson, Gunna Go Never Goes, Debra Adelaide, ed., *Cutting the Cord: Stories of Children, Love and Loss*, Random House, Sydney, 1998

Jeri Kroll, The Not-So-Good Mother, Debra Adelaide, ed., *Cutting the Cord: Stories of Children, Love and Loss*, Random House, Sydney, 1998

Robert Lawlor, *Voices of the First Day: Awakening in the Aboriginal Dreamtime*, Inner Traditions International, Rochester VT, 1991

Elizabeth Noble, *Primal Connections*, Simon & Schuster, New York NY, 1993
The author wishes to thank Elizabeth Noble for her research on this subject.

Dr John Quintner, Taking the Cake, *The Medical Observer*, 26 November 1999

Chapter 5

David Chamberlain, *The Mind of Your Newborn Baby*, North Atlantic Books, Berkeley CA, 1998

Deva Daricha, *Body Transformation: Transformation of the Body into Light*, unpublished manuscript, April 1996

Leslie Feher, *The Psychology of Birth: The Foundation of Human Personality*, Souvenir Press, London UK, 1980

Sigmund Freud, *Problems of Anxiety*, Hogarth Press, London UK, 1936

Stanislav Grof, *Beyond the Brain: Birth, death, and Transcendence in Psychotherapy*, State University of New York Press, Albany NY, 1985

Arthur Janov, *Imprints: The Lifelong Effects of the Birth Experience*, Coward-McCann, Inc., New York NY, 1983

RD Laing, *The Facts of Life*, Penguin Books, London UK, 1976

Frederick Leboyer, *Birth Without Violence*, Knopf, New York NY, 1975

Francis Mott, *The Nature of the Self: The Human Mind Rediscovered as a Specific Instance of a Universal Configuration Governing all Integration*, Allan Wingate, London UK, 1959

Elizabeth Noble, *Primal Connections: How our experiences from conception to birth influence our emotions, behavior, and health*, Simon & Schuster, New York NY, 1993

Michel Odent, *The Scientification of Love*, Free Association Books, London UK, 1999

Joseph Chilton Pearce, *Evolution's End:Claiming the Potential of Our Intelligence*, Harper, San Francisco CA, 1992

Otto Rank, *The Trauma of Birth*, Routledge, London UK, 1929

Wilhelm Reich, *The Function of the Orgasm*, Simon & Schuster, New York NY, 1973

Chapter 6

Alan Gardiner, *Egyptian Grammar: being an introduction to the study of hieroglyphics*, Oxford University Press, 1957

RD Laing, *The Facts of Life*, Penguin Books, London UK, 1976

In Chapter 7, Cutting the Umbilical Cord, well-known British

psychiatrist RD Laing wrote about the cutting of the umbilical cord
as a source of birth trauma for the infant.

Dr Christopher J Millar, *My Memory of Birth*, Long Point Publishers,
Creswick VIC, 1984

Chapter 7

Jeannine Parvati Baker, Lotus Birth fully bloomed, *Mothering Magazine*,
Summer 1983

Clair Lotus Day, Keeping the unity of pregnancy, letter, 1975

Pacia Sallomi, The amazing placenta: The tree of life, *Mothering Magazine*, Summer 1983

Alice Scholes, The Lotus placenta, *Homebirth Australia* Newsletter
No. 21, O'Connor ACT, Winter 1989

Chapter 8

Dr Sarah Buckley, Lotus Birth: a ritual for our times, *Pregnancy*, Spring
1998

Christal, Zephyr, letter to Clair Lotus Day, 4 October 1975

Contributors

Jeannine Parvati Baker is the mother of six consciously born children, five of them lotus babies, and grandmother of one lotus underwater freeborn baby (in 1995). She is the co-founder of Six Directions, a non-profit educational corporation devoted to optimal personal, family and planetary health. She is the founder of Hygieia College Mystery School in Lay Midwifery & Womancraft; editorial board member of the Primal Renaissance; and a keynote speaker for IPA, APPPAH, NOCIRC, Birth, Education, Health, Herb, and Women Conferences around the world. She is the author of *Prenatal Yoga and Natural Birth* and *Hygieia: A Woman's Herbal* and other publications. Read her stories in her *Lotus Birth Information Packet* or the publications listed under Contacts.

Anne Blanch had a midwifery practice in Tasmania for 17 years. A traditional home birth midwife, she attended over 700 births. She was instrumental in establishing the birth centre at Launceston hospital. She has four children, three of whom were born at home.

Sarah Buckley is a Brisbane GP with a special interest in birth and parenting. She has written numerous articles about birth and parenting for journals, magazines and newspapers. She is a mother of four.

Christal was one of the first women who followed Clair Lotus Day's example of choosing Lotus Birth for her baby and described her experiences in a letter to Clair in 1975.

Deva Daricha, BA BEd (Mon.) TPTC, read History, Philosophy and Education at Monash University before teaching Philosophy for 13 years. He left academic life to establish Greenwood Lane Centre, a residential spiritual community, with his wife Shivam Rachana. Together they direct the Centre for Human Transformation in the Yarra Valley, Victoria and have jointly authored *The Tantric Path*. An initiated shaman, Daricha is the originator of the Body Transformation Process, which is an exploration and healing of the soul's journey into conscious embodiment, as well as the five-day retreat 'Dying to Live', an examination of the process of conscious dying and the recovery of the vision of one's soul.

Clair Lotus Day, who described herself as 'a clairvoyant, nurse and teacher', was one of the first who believed that the umbilical cord should not be cut at birth but allowed to fall off naturally with the placenta at around the seventh day after birth, the time when the umbilical stump of a cord that has been cut will usually shrivel and fall away. Clair called this way of birth 'Lotus Birth' and developed elaborate written material describing the spiritual benefits of this method and the psychological harm which may result from cutting the cord. She is regarded by many as the 'Mother of Lotus Birth'. Clair has since passed away but her spirit lives on in the practice of Lotus Birth.

Trish Douglas lives with her partner John in Bayside, Melbourne, where she enjoys the adventure and ongoing learning of being with her lotus-born son Tristan in his unfolding development. She is involved in her local community and the activities of the ICSM.

Sunderai Felich is an independent Childbirth Educator and Doula with 20 years' experience in children's and women's health. Sunderai is Vice Principal of ICSM and co-ordinator of Dial a Doula, a service for women in the greater Melbourne metropolitan area.

Naomi Hermann, one of the first women to choose a Lotus Birth for her baby, studied Natural Hygiene and worked at the Utopia Health Centre in Texas.

Branwen Hooke was born in 1976 and grew up in the mountains outside Melbourne. She is a singer and a mother. Her daughter, Ella Shiani, was born in May 1999.

Janet Ireland works and lives in Melbourne. She has practised midwifery since 1967. During the last four years she has set up a busy private practice which she runs from her home in Hampton. Jan also enjoys working at Wattle Park House with Peter Lucas (GP) and Jennie Teskey (RM). A large proportion of births she attends are at home. Her special interests include EBAC (empowering birth after Caesarean section), water birth and siblings at birth.

Katrina Japp has been associated with the Centre for Human Transformation as a student for a many years. She gave birth at the Centre to her lotus-born daughter Ela-rose. She has another child, son Jasha.

Davini Joy is a founding member and director of the International College of Spiritual Midwifery (ICSM). She is a professional actress, having worked in Australian Film and Television for nearly 18 years. Davini has studied Breath Therapy, Tantra and Women's Mysteries. She teaches workshops for Teenage Girls, The Nature of This Flower is to Bloom, and Bodybizness for women of all ages and offers individual sessions in Breath Therapy, Counselling and Bodybizness. Davini lives with her fiance Peter Malcolm and is the proud mother of Satchi (8) and Zak (4) – her greatest treasures and greatest teachers. Both of her sons were lotus-born at home, into water. As this book goes to print, Davini is expecting twins (due in early 2001).

Anand Khushi, BSc (Ethnology/Clinical Psychology) and a director of ICSM, trained at the Centre for Human Transformation in Body Transformation, Rebirthing, Tantra and Women's Mysteries. She birthed her lotus water baby in bliss at home nine years ago. A sound healer, Khushi specialises in assisting women to remember how to give voice to the feminine. As western humans drift further into practising cold-blooded, reptilian conception and birthing rituals, Khushi anchors herself, with a strong community of other women and men, in the knowing that we must respect and nurture our mammalian instincts if we are to love and care for our children and to evolve further.

Jennifer VanLaanen-Smit, aka Mango Mama, describes herself as a domestic goddess, mother of three, and nature sprite. She is the author of *Natural Parenting* and lives in Hawaii.

Simone Lukacs is mother of two Lotus Birth children, Seireadan and Madeleine, and was intuitively drawn to birthing this way. Her children's physical robustness, mental alertness, emotional honesty and spiritual integrity confirm Lotus Birth's many benefits at every stage of their development. Simone is a writer by profession, and a keen gardener, quilter and photographer.

Dr Christopher Millar, MD, explored the experience of having his umbilical cord cut in primal therapy. He recorded his experiences in a book, *My Memory of Birth* (Long Point Publishers, Creswick VIC, 1984). 'Twenty years ago while still a medical student I pursued experiential learning with primal therapist Graham Farrant. It was such a revelation that I am still sorting through the material I unearthed then, as well as continuing on my journey.'

Michel Odent is well known as the obstetrician who introduced, in a French state hospital, the concepts of homelike birthing rooms and birthing pools. He was educated in the 50s as a surgeon, and may be regarded as one of the last real general surgeons. At the end of his hospital career he practised as a home birth midwife. Michel Odent is the founder of the Primal Health research centre in London, whose objective is to study correlations between what happens during the 'primal period' (from conception until the first birthday) and health and behaviour later in life. The primal research data bank holds hundreds of references and abstracts of studies published in scientific and medical journals. He is the author of 50 scientific papers and 10 books published in 19 languages.

Karyn Patterson has a Diploma of Antenatal Education (1984) and completed Module II of Body Transformation in 1996, as well as studying various other bodywork techniques. She works as a midwife in the traditional sense. She has three children, Alyosha, Miranda, and Raphael, born four weeks after Karyn was introduced to Lotus Birth in a Women's Mysteries group. Ten years on, Raphael continues to display an unusual sense of completeness and a striking concern for justice of individuals.

Renuka Potter, MA, is a transpersonal psychologist with a counselling and bodywork practice in Clifton Hill, Melbourne. For fifteen years she taught undergraduate Psychology and Women's Studies at tertiary level. She was co-author of the *Birthing Services Review* for Southwest Victoria 1988. Living with Aboriginal people in the 1970s at Yuendumu, 260 km northwest of Alice Springs, opened her to the exploration of extra dimensions of life. She has given birth naturally to two great children and has meditated for twenty-five years.

Bodhi Priti is a founding member and director of the International College of Spiritual Midwifery. Bodhi has been working in the field of women's health for the past 10 years as a practitioner of the Body Transformation process, a breath therapist and a Natural Fertility counsellor. She works with girls and women to reclaim the inner knowledge of their bodies and their fertility as their birthright. Bodhi birthed her two daughters at home in water; both were Lotus Births.

Shivam Rachana is the founding Principal of the International College of Spiritual Midwifery (ICSM). She has 30 years' teaching experience and has worked in the area of women's health, particularly childbirth, since the 1970s. Rachana has been attending home births since 1977, attended Australia's first waterbirth and introduced Lotus Birth into Australia. She is a trainer of rebirthers and Tantra and the author of *The Tantric Path*. The originator of the initiatory Women's Mysteries five-day retreats, Rachana is a much-loved and respected teacher and her students practise throughout Australia and New Zealand.

Kerry Radford practises midwifery in a public hospital and in an independent community midwifery group. She continues to expand her awareness and knowledge of natural childbirth, and feels passionate about holistic midwifery care to enhance the journey of childbirth for the mother and her baby. Her understanding of the significance of the birth process for the baby has led her to be a committed advocate for gentle conscious childbirth. She is the mother of five wonderful children.

Pacia Sallomi is an associate editor for *Mothering Magazine* and a midwife practising in Albuquerque, New Mexico.

Alice Scholes worked as a traditional midwife in NSW for more than 15 years. She was a pioneer of water birth and a leading light in the conscious birth movement.

Kairava Shan-Ra has had three Lotus and waterbirths (two sons and one daughter). She is a founding member and director of ICSM. Kairava works extensively in the women's field, teaching sacred dance, and is the founder of the Ecstatic Dance Program. Trained in breathwork, Body Transformation, Postural Integration and Zen Bodywork, Kairava is a teacher at the Centre for Human Transformation and has run a practice of bodywork and counselling for over 10 years. She has a BA in Psychology and English Literature.

Soni Stecker, Dip PW&E, RMIT, works as a freelance editor, writer and translator. She has an MA in Transpersonal Psychology from Antioch University, San Francisco, and a certificate in Swedish-Esalen massage. She is a life member of ICSM and has a passion for writing and publishing, especially on transpersonal topics.

Further reading and resources

The following publications may be helpful in gaining more understanding of the birthing process and its implications in our lives.

Suzanne Arms, *Immaculate Deception II: A Fresh Look at Childbirth*, Celestial Arts, Berkeley CA, 1994

Jeannine Parvati Baker, *Prenatal Yoga and Natural Birth*, Freestone Publishing Co, Monroe UT, 1974/1986

Jeannine Parvati Baker and Frederick Baker, *Conscious Conception: Elemental Journey through the Labyrinth of Sexuality*, Freestone Publishing Co, Monroe UT, 1986

Janet Balaskas, *Active Birth*, Unwin Paperbacks, London UK, 1983

Maggie Banks, *Home Birth Bound – Mending the broken weave*, Birthspirit Books, Hamilton NZ, 2000

Maggie Banks, *Breech Birth, Woman-Wise*, Birthspirit Books, Hamilton NZ, 1998

Beverley Lawrence Beech, *Choosing a Waterbirth*, AIMS, London UK, 1998

Beverley Lawrence Beech and Jan Robinson, *Ultrasound Unsound?*, AIMS, London UK, 1990

David Chamberlain, *Babies Remember Birth: And Other Extraordinary Scientific Discoveries about the Mind and Personality of your Newborn*, Ballantine Books, New York NY, 1988/1990

Nancy Wainer Cohen, *Open Season: A Survival Guide for Natural Childbirth and VBAC in the 90s*, Bergin and Garvey, Westport CT, 1991

Elizabeth Davis, *Heart and Hands: A Midwife's Guide to Pregnancy and Birth*, Photos by Suzanne Arms, Celestial Arts, Berkeley CA, 1997

Grantly Dick-Read, *Childbirth without Fear*, Harper, New York NY, 1944/1994

Bruce Flamm, *Birth After Cesarean: The Medical Facts*, US, 1990

Robbie Davis-Floyd, *Birth as an American Rite of Passage*, University of California Press, Berkeley CA, 1992

M Enkin, M Kierse, M Renfrew, J Nielson, *Guide to Effective Care in Pregnancy and Childbirth*, Oxford University Press, Oxford UK, 1995

Ina May Gaskin, *Spiritual Midwifery*, The Book Publishing Company, Summertown TN, 1990

Henci Goer, *Obstetric Myths vs Research Realities: A Guide to the Medical Literature*, Bergin and Garvey, Westport CT, 1995

Ronald Goldman, *Circumcision: The Hidden Trauma*, Vanguard, Boston MA, 1997

Elisabeth B Hallett, *Soul Trek: Meeting our Children on the Way to Birth*, Light Hearts Publishing, Hamilton MT, 1995

Barbara Harper, *Gentle Birth Choices: A Guide to Making Informed Decisions*, Inner Traditions, Rochester VT, 1994

Jessica Johnson and Michel Odent, *We are all Water Babies*, Celestial Arts, Berkeley CA, 1995

Karr-Morse and Wiley, *Ghosts from the Nursery*, US, 1998

Sheila Kitzinger, *Your Baby, Your Way: Making Pregnancy Decisions and Birth Plans*, Pantheon Books, London UK, 1987

Sheila Kitzinger, *Pregnancy and Childbirth*, Pantheon Books, London UK, 1997

Marshall Klaus, John Kennell, and Phyllis Klaus, *Bonding: Building the Foundations of Secure Attachment and Independence*, Addison-Wesley, Reading MA, 1995

Frederick Leboyer, *Birth without Violence*, Alfred Knopf, New York NY, 1975/1996

Jean Liedloff, *The Continuum Concept*, Warner Books, New York NY, 1977

Benig Mauger, *Reclaiming the Spirituality of Birth*, Healing Arts Press, Rochester VT, 2000

Ashley Montague, *Touch: The Human Significance of the Skin*, Harper and Row, New York NY, 1978

Elizabeth Noble, *Childbirth with Insight*, Houghton-Mifflin, Boston MA, 1983

Elizabeth Noble, *Essential Exercises for the Childbearing Year*, New Life Images, Harwich MA, 1995

Elizabeth Noble, *Primal Connections: How Our Experiences from Conception to Birth influence our Emotions, Behavior and Health*, Fireside, Simon and Schuster, New York NY, 1993

Michel Odent, *Birth Reborn*, Pantheon, New York NY, 1984/1994

Michel Odent, *The Nature of Birth and Breastfeeding*, ACE Graphics, Sydney, 1992

Michel Odent, *The Scientification of Love*, Free Association Books, London UK, 1999

Claudia Panuthos, *Transformation through Birth: A Woman's Guide*, Greenwood Publishing Group, Westport CT, 1984

Joseph Chilton Pearce, *Magical Child: Rediscovering Nature's Plan for our Children*, Dutton, New York NY, 1977

Joseph Chilton Pearce, *Evolution's End: Reclaiming the Potential of our Intelligence*, Harper, San Francisco CA, 1992

Elizabeth Clare Prophet, *Nurturing Your Baby's Soul*, Summit University Press, Corwin Springs MT, 1998

William and Martha Sears, *The Baby Book: Birth to Two Years*, US, 1993

Jean Sutton and Pauline Scott, *Optimal Foetal Positioning*, NZ, 1995

Thomas Verny with John Kelly, *The Secret Life of the Unborn Child*, Dell, New York NY, 1981/1986

Marsden Wagner, *Pursuing the Birth Machine: The Search for Appropriate Birth Technology*, ACE Graphics, Camperdown NSW, 1994

Videos

Birth Into Being, 25mins, US, 1999. Order from: Global Maternal Health Association, PO Box 1400, Wilsonville OR, US 97070

Birth in the Squatting Position, 10 mins, Brazil, 1990

Channel for a New Life, Elizabeth Noble, 37 mins, US, 1988

Gentle Birth Choices, Barbara Harper, 47 mins, US, 1995

Giving Birth: Challenges and Choices, Suzanne Arms, 35 mins, US, 1998

Water and Birth, Janet Balaskas, 58 mins, UK, 1992

Journals and magazines

AIMS journal, $25 per year, Association for Improvement in Maternity
Services, London, 163 Liverpool Street, London N1 ORF, UK

Journal of Pre- and Perinatal Psychology and Health, US$75 per year,
e-mail: apppah@aol.com

Mothering, US$18.95 per year,
e-mail: subscriptions@mothering.com

Contacts

(Website addresses correct at time of publication.)

International College of Spiritual Midwifery
144 Barkers Road, Hawthorn, Victoria 3122
Ph: + 61 3 9818 1177
Email: icsm@womenofspirit.asn.au
www.womenofspirit.asn.au

Register of Lotus Birth babies in Australia
Parents and midwives: if you would like your story to become part
of the Lotus Birth collection, or would like to add your Lotus Birth
baby's name to the list, phone Rachana on:
+61 3 5965 2325
or write to:
Shivam Rachana, PO Box 233, Yarra Glen, Victoria 3775
E-mail: golden@xtreme.net.au

Centre for Human Transformation
PO Box 233, Yarra Glen, Victoria 3775, Australia
Telephone: +61 3 5965 2022
Fax: +61 3 5965 2588
E-mail: golden@xtreme.net.au

Dr Sarah Buckley
Dr Sarah Buckley has written numerous articles about birth and
parenting for journals, magazines and newspapers and is happy to
share her experiences and expertise.
Telephone: +61 7 3202 9052
~~E-mail: N.Lennox@spmed.uq.edu.au~~

Jeannine Parvati Baker
> *Lotus Birth Information Packet*
> available from: JP Baker, 40 No State Street, Joseph UT
> 84739-1207 USA
> (US$11 postpaid)

Other publications:
> *Prenatal Yoga & Natural Birth* (1974/1986). The first book (possibly
> world-wide) in print with a story of Lotus Birth. Jeannine Par-
> vati Baker had been ordained by Clair Lotus Day to carry her
> message to the world. (Second edn. published the same year as
> *Conscious Conception*.)
>
> *Hygieia: A Woman's Herbal* (first edition 1978). This book, having
> sold over 100,000 copies, possibly spread the Lotus Birth
> word more than any other US publication.
>
> *Conscious Conception: Elemental Journey through the Labyrinth of
> Sexuality* (with Frederick Baker, 1986)

For a complete list of publications by JP Baker, see the website:
http://www.freestone.org

Mango Mama's Natural Parenting Site
> http://www.mangomama.org
> or
> http://www.naturalparenting.org

Established by Jennifer VanLaanen-Smit; information on natural
childbirth. This site addresses everyday childcare issues from a
natural perspective, and supports parents who parent outside the
mainstream – from pre-conception to home schooling. A good
place to turn to when intuition tells you that the standard advice is
not right for you.

International College of Spiritual Midwifery (ICSM)

History

The International College of Spiritual Midwifery had its beginnings in 1988, when a group of five women gathered together for five days to explore the depths of their individual and collective connections. They wanted to know more about living in a woman's body, with the ever-changing events and challenges, surprises and wonders it provided. They looked to live their female potential to its fullest. What they found were many gaps in their knowledge. They committed to filling those gaps, and to embody as fully as they possibly could the woman's journey.

So successful was this first gathering in its capacity to hold and nurture the deep feminine that many, many more gatherings have followed. In August 1997 the International College of Spiritual Midwifery officially opened at The Queen Victoria Women's Centre in Melbourne.

Today ICSM is a community of women, working together in an organic and dynamic way, that provides a range of programs for women and their families. It is a unique and practical example of women in community living ancient women's knowledge in a modern context. ICSM programs are held throughout Australia and New Zealand.

Aims

The International College of Spiritual Midwifery aims to awaken the spirit of midwifery and promote its art.

We aim to provide the opportunity for women to undertake the journey to freedom, through information and making fully informed choices.

To achieve this goal we hold radically innovative seminars, workshops and individual sessions and provide access to internationally recognised teachers and practitioners.

We provide a comprehensive package of knowledge, support and practical training for natural pregnancy, birth and parenting.

We provide midwives, doctors and birth attendants with the opportunity to learn techniques that will enrich their own experience and enable them to become more valuable resources for birthing families.

Vision

The teaching of the ICSM is centered on returning women to the sovereignty of their own bodies, and to the inherent power within.

For as women, we are part of a continuum, our ancestors live within us, just as we will live within our descendants. Our mothers arrived from our grandmother's womb carrying the ovum that would become us.

As a woman's life traverses its many directions and turning points, including sexuality, ovulation, menstruation, conception, pregnancy, birth, lactation, motherhood, menopause and grandmotherhood, pathways are created to allow for awareness, growth and transformation.

Spiritual Midwifery reclaims a woman's power in her own process. It allows women the chance to remember how to listen to their bodies, and trust in their ability to respond to this new intelligence. In this, a deep inner knowing pervades and strength is brought to all undertakings.

The more a woman is able to be herself as a woman, the more she is able to be with other women as they travel the rich and sometimes challenging landscape of womanhood. Hence the original meaning of midwife – with woman.

When women live their lives in this way balance can be present on the Earth. This way of living gives men a point of reference with the feminine that invokes and insists on their highest potential also being realised.

Children who are born of and cared for by such women and men grow strong in their own sense of responsibility. It is in this that we create the future we wish for our children and the generations to come.

Programs provided by ICSM

- Introduction to Spiritual Midwifery
- Fertility awareness
- Conscious Conception
- Healing Birth Trauma
- Childbirth Preparation
- Dial a Doula Service
- Doula trainings
- Physiotherapy
- Rebirthing and Breath Therapy
- Body Transformation Process
- Women's Healing Circle
- Relationship counselling
- Healing Sound Therapy
- Ecstatic Dance
- Women, Power and Birth Forums
- Women's Mysteries one-day seminars
- Women's Mysteries five-day retreats

Contact Addresses
www.humantransformation.com.au
www.womenofspirit.asn.au
(International College of Spiritual Midwifery)
www.waterbirth.org
Email address for Dr. Sarah Buckley
sarahjbuckley@uqconnect.net

Dial a Doula

Doula is a Greek word meaning 'woman care giver'. A Doula provides physical, emotional and informational support to women and their families before, during and after childbirth. A Doula recognises birth as a key experience that the mother will remember all her life. She understands the physiology of birth and the emotional needs of a woman in labour. A Doula assists women and their partners to prepare for and carry out their plans for the birth of their baby. She can stay by the side of the labouring woman throughout the entire labour and facilitate communication between the labouring woman, her partner and clinical caregivers.

A Doula provides: labour support, massage, childcare, relaxation techniques, breastfeeding support and domestic support. Studies from around the world show that women attended at birth by a Doula have a much greater chance of a normal and satisfying birth experience.

Benefits of having a trained Doula include: 50% reduction in Caesarean rate, 25% shorter labour, 60% reduction in epidural requests, 40% reduction in oxytocin use, 30% reduction in analgesia use and 40% reduction in forceps delivery. (*Mothering the Mother: How a Doula can help you have a shorter, easier and healthier birth*, Klaus, Kennell and Klaus 1993.)

Established by the International College of Spiritual Midwifery (ICSM) in March 1998, Dial a Doula provides a passionate and expansive network of women who support other women and their families before, during and after childbirth.

Melbourne metropolitan region and surrounding locations
Telephone: 03 9654 3737   Mobile: 0401 626 883

'Because the more a mother is cared for the more easily she can care for her baby.'

Centre for Human Transformation

The Centre for Human Transformation is located in the beautiful Yarra Valley, one hour's drive from Melbourne. It provides leading edge programs for professional training, personal exploration and spiritual unfolding. Practitioners from its courses practise throughout Australia, and it is now developing a team of national trainers who will shortly expand the work internationally. CHT is a sister organisation of ICSM, which developed out of CHT's activities.

Over the past 15 years the Centre has developed profound, innovative programs in Women's Mysteries, Shamanism and cross-cultural spiritual exchange with indigenous peoples, Men's work, and the Body Transformation process, as well as Rebirthing and Breath therapy. These latter two prepare people to work as natural healers using breath, touch, sound and the energies of Grace to bring ease to the body, mind, emotions and soul.

A recent addition to the programs – 'Dying to Live' – is an examination of conscious living and dying and the recovery of the incarnatory vision of one's soul.

The Centre's understanding of Tantric Sexuality is articulated in *The Tantric Path* by Deva Daricha and Shivam Rachana, and the programs which are based on these understandings have been acclaimed by participants and acknowledged internationally.

Directed by Deva Daricha and Shivam Rachana, the programs are offered via a national teaching program, details of which can be found on the ICSM website or by enquiry to:

Centre for Human Transformation
PO Box 233, Yarra Glen, Victoria 3775, Australia
Telephone: +61 3 5965 2325
Fax: +61 3 5965 2588
E-mail: golden@xtreme.net.au

ORDER FORM

Please send me

_____ copies of *Lotus Birth*

at A$ 29.95 per copy (includes GST)   _____

postage and handling at

$5.50 per book (in Australia)   _____

A$10.00 per book (overseas)   _____

Total amount   _____

Name _____

Address _____

_____

_____

_____

Payment enclosed

_____ Cheque (made out to: Greenwood Press)

_____ International Money Order (made out to: Greenwood Press)

_____ Credit card no. _____

Expiry date _____ / _____

Name on credit card _____

Signature _____

Please mail to: Greenwood Press
                    PO Box 233
                    Yarra Glen, Victoria 3775
                    Australia